World Chronology Series

ENGLAND

A CHRONOLOGY AND FACT BOOK

1485-1973

Compiled and Edited by
ROBERT I. VEXLER

1974
OCEANA PUBLICATIONS, INC.
Dobbs Ferry, New York

Library of Congress Cataloging in Publication Data

Vexler, Robert I
    England: a chronology and fact book, 1485-1973.

    (World chronology series)
    Bibliography: p.
    1. Great Britain--History--Chronology. 2. Great
Britain--History--Sources. I. Title.
DA34.V5   942   73-17067
ISBN 0-379-16306-3

Manufactured in the United States of America

TABLE OF CONTENTS

EDITOR'S FOREWORD

The aim of this and subsequent volumes in the <u>World</u> <u>Chronology</u> <u>Series</u> is to provide basic material indicating the domestic as well as foreign developments of each nation. The material has been selected in order to illustrate the important aspects of English history during the past five centuries.

This research tool has been compiled for the student. The advent of the Tudors in 1485 has been selected as the starting point of this chronology because this is, in the opinion of the editor, the true beginning of modern English History. Emphasis has been placed on England with factors concerning Scotland and Ireland chosen which bear directly on English developments.

The purpose of these works is to make available some of the pertinent facts and key documents as well as a critical bibliography which will help the student to investigate additional and conflicting materials. The works cited may not necessarily be available in all small libraries, but they have been selected from among the newer ones or those which have been reprinted because of their significance to the study of various aspects of British History.

Robert I. Vexler
Briarcliff College

To my wife Francine

whose help and suggestions

made this book possible

THE TUDOR PERIOD

1485   August 22. Henry Tudor and his forces defeated King
            Richard III at the Battle of Bosworth Field.

            November 7. The coronation of Henry VII took place.

1486   January 18. Henry married Elizabeth of York, merging
            the Lancastrian and Yorkist claims to the throne, only
            after Parliament had recognized Henry as King.

            September 20. Prince Arthur, first son and heir of
            Henry VII, was born.

1487   November 9. The Parliament met. It was to create the
            Star Chamber during this session.

1488   July 28. The Breton army, including English, German,
            Spanish and Navarese troops, was defeated by the French
            at St. Aubin de Cormier.

1489   February 10. The Treaty of Redon was signed between
            England and Brittany.

            March 27. Treaty of Medina del Campo was signed be-
            tween England and Spain. Henry was granted a Spanish
            marriage for his son. The remainder of the terms were
            favorable to the Spanish.

1490   A Trade Treaty was signed with Denmark.

1491   June 29. Prince Henry, future King, was born.

1492   November 3. French and English signed the Peace
            of Etaples.

1496   March 5. Letters Patent were issued to John Cabot to
            sail to the East, West and North. New letters patent
            were issued to him on February 3, 1498.

1497   June 18. Henry VII ratified the Marriage Treaty between
            Prince Arthur and the Infanta of Spain, which had been
            signed October 1, 1496.

October 5. Perkin Warbeck, pretender to the throne, was brought before Henry VII and the Council. He confessed his crimes against the State in leading an uprising against Henry.

1499   Fall. Erasmus of Rotterdam went to Oxford University where he stayed until December.

November 28. The Earl of Warwick was executed for conspiracy against the throne.

1501   November 15. Prince Arthur and Catharine of Aragon were married.

1502   April 2. Prince Arthur died. Henry Tudor became heir to his father's throne.

June 19. A treaty was signed with the Emperor Maximilian, granting him ₺10,000 towards the Turkish war in return for a promise not to aid the English rebels.

August 7. Margaret Tudor married James IV of Scotland.

1503   February 18. Henry was created Prince of Wales.

June 23. Prince Henry and Princess Catharine were betrothed. Pope Julius granted a dispensation for their marriage.

1505   June 27. Prince Henry denounced the marriage contract with Catharine.

1506   February 9. The Treaty of Windsor was signed with King Philip of Castile, who had accidentally landed on English soil on January 16, because of storm. It was an offensive and defensive alliance.

April 30. The Malus Intercursus was arranged between Netherlands and England, permitting English woolens to be sold wholesale in the provinces.

1509   April 21. Henry VII died. He was succeeded by Henry VIII.

June 11. Henry VIII married Catharine of Aragon.

1510   November 17. A treaty was signed with Aragon, pledging
            England to go to war with France the following April.

1513   April. Henry invaded France.

1514   July 10. A peace treaty was signed with France. Henry's
            sister, Mary, was to marry Louis XII, whose wife died
            January 9.

1515   Thomas Wolsey became Cardinal and Lord Chancellor.

            April 5. A treaty was signed between England and France.
            which enabled King Francis of France to invade Italy.

1516   Thomas More's Utopia was published.

1517   October 31. Martin Luther posted his 95 Theses on the
            door of the Cathedral Church which led to the Reforma-
            tion.

1518   October 2. Wolsey arranged a Treaty of universal peace
            including England, France, the Empire, the Papacy and
            Spain.

1519   Duke of Richmond and Somerset (Henry VIII's illegitimate
            son) was born to Elizabeth Blount.

1520   June 4 - 24. Meeting of Henry VIII and Francis I of
            France was held on the Field of the Cloth of Gold in France,
            which illustrated the friendship of the two nations, although
            nothing of major significance was achieved.

1521   November 24. Wolsey signed a league with Emperor
            Charles V that if Francis did not conclude peace with
            the Emperor, Henry was to declare war on France. In
            addition, the Lady Mary was to be married to Charles.

1522   June 19. Henry and Charles V met at Windsor to conclude
            arrangements for a struggle against France.

            August. The English, under Henry Howard, Earl of
            Surrey, invaded France.

1525   August 14. A truce between France and England was
            signed.

1527

April. It became clear to Henry that he was a bachelor because of the Biblical injunctions against his marriage to his brother's widow. Anne Boleyn had caught the King's fancy.

April 30. Three Treaties with France were signed at Westminster indicating that after peace and an alliance was arranged between the two powers, the Emperor would be forced to enter the League on the threat of war. Francis was to pay a perpetual pension to England.

May 6. Charles' troops sacked Rome and captured the Pope.

May 17. Clerical Court was opened by Wolsey and Waltham to enquire into the royal marriage. The proceedings were closed on May 31.

December 23. Pope Clement granted a provisional dispensation for Henry VIII's remarriage should his union to Catharine prove to be invalid.

1529

May 31. The Legatine Court was opened by Cardinal Campeggio at the Blackfriars. Catharine appeared on June 18 and protested against the competence of the Legates.

July 23. Campeggio adjourned the court, as the Consistory was on vacation until October 1.

August 9. Henry issued writs for Parliament to meet on November 3 to deal with the issue of his divorce. In addition, on advice of Thomas Cranmer, Henry decided to submit the issue to the universities of Europe.

October 16. Wolsey was ordered to give up the seal because of disappointment with the manner in which he was handling the divorce case.

1531

February 11. Henry VIII was given the title of Supreme Head of the Church of England.

1532

March 19. The bill to abolish annate payments to the Papacy was passed.

May 15. The Convocation of the Clergy accepted three articles by which the clergy completely submitted the Church to the State. The Church was to approve a change in the clerical requirements.

1533   January 25. Sometime about this date, Henry and Anne Boleyn were secretly married.

March 30. Thomas Cranmer was consecrated Archbishop of Canterbury.

April 23. The Dunstable judgment by an English Court declared the marriage of Henry and Catharine null and void.

June 1. Ann Boleyn was crowned Queen in Westminster Abbey.

July 11. Sentence was announced against Henry along with his excommunication which was pronounced at Rome.

September 7. Elizabeth was born to Henry and Anne Boleyn.

1534   January. The final severance between the Church of England and Rome was effected.

March 16. An act for restraint of Annates was passed, prohibiting procurement of bulls or briefs from Rome.

March 30. An act was passed forbidding payments of Peters pence and other pensions or fees to Rome. In addition, an act was passed requiring submission of the clergy to the King. A Commission was appointed by the King to reform the Canon Law. There could be no appeals to Rome, but there could be an appeal from the archbishop's court to the King in Chancery.

The Act of Succession was passed vesting the succession of the crown in the heirs of Henry by Anne Boleyn. It also declared Henry's marriage to Catharine invalid and his marriage with Anne valid.

April 13. A Royal Commission was issued to Dr. George Browne and Dr. Hilsey to investigate all friars' houses.

May 11. Peace was arranged between England and Scotland.

November. The Act of Supremacy was passed declaring the King to be the Supreme Head of the Church of England. It was to be in force for 20 years.

1535   January. A Church Council was held where the Bishops
                were forced to recognize the King as the Supreme head
                of the Church, and that he could act at will in regard to
                their appointment and removal.

                July 1. The trial of Sir Thomas More for treason was held
                because he supposedly wanted to deprive the King of the
                title of Supreme Head of the Church of England. More
                was executed on July 6.

1536   January 7. Catharine of Aragon died.

                May 15. Anne Boleyn was brought to trial on charges of
                indiscretion and disloyalty, many of which were prefabri-
                cated.

                May 17. Cranmer declared Henry and Anne's marriage
                null and void.

                May 19. Anne was executed.

                May 30. Henry married Jane Seymour.

                July 11. The Ten Articles were proclaimed to assure
                uniformity in the Church.

1537   February 9. Reginald Cardinal Pole was created _legatus_
                a latene and was sent north to offer aid to Catholic insur-
                gents in England. His mission failed.

                October 12. Prince Edward was born.

                October 24. Queen Jane (Seymour) died.

1538   September 5. Cromwell issued a series of injunctions
                leading to further religious change.

                November. Henry issued a proclamation, establishing
                censorship over English books and indicating that only
                properly trained clerics should discuss the sacrament.

  December 17. A Papal Bull excommunicating Henry for his
                action against the Church was issued.

1539   May. The Six Articles Act was passed.

Parliament also passed an Act, "abolishing Diversity of
Opinion" with severe penalties. An act was also passed
granting the King and his heirs all monasteries surrendered or forfeited since February 5, 1536, and providing that all monasteries which are dissolved or relinquished be vested in the King.

October 4. A Marriage Treaty was signed at Hampton
Court between Henry and Anne of Cleves.

1540   January 6. Henry and Anne of Cleves were married.

June 10. Thomas Cromwell was arrested and sent to
the Tower. On June 29, a bill of attainder was passed
condemning Cromwell to suffer as a heretic or a traitor.
He was also forced to give evidence which would enable
Henry to rid himself of his ugly wife.

July 9. The United Convocations of Canterbury and
York declared the King's marriage to be null and void.

July 28. Henry married Catharine Howard.

July 29. Cromwell was executed.

1541   May 6. All Curates and parishoners were commanded
to set up Bibles of the largest volume in the Churches.

1542   January 16. Parliament was opened. Shortly thereafter, it passed an act of attainder against the Queen,
Catharine Howard, and Lady Rochford. Henry VIII
had received evidence on November 2 of Catharine's
grave misconduct before their marriage.

February 13. Catharine Howard was executed.

1543   May. The King's Book was issued, giving the formu-
lary for the Anglican Church which was in many ways
a strict and explicit manifesto of Catholic orthodoxy.

June 22. Henry sent an ultimatum to France, so framed
as to be a declaration of war.

July 1. The Treaties of Greenwich were signed with the
Scots. The first was a treaty of peace, and the second

a treaty of marriage between Prince Edward, 6, and Mary Queen of Scotland. They never went fully into effect. The Scottish Parliament used the pretext that their merchant ships were taken by the English at sea to break the treaty on December 11.

July 12. Henry married Catharine Parr.

1544

July 14. Henry crossed the English Channel to Calais to superintend, but not to lead, the army.

September 18. The Treaty of Crespy was signed whereby Emperor Charles made peace with France.

November 19. The Pope issued a summons for a General Council of Trent in the Spring of 1545 to deal with the Protestant Reformation.

1546

June 7. A Peace Treaty between England and France was signed.

1547

January 28. Henry VIII died. His death was kept a secret for several days.

January 31. Lord Chancellor Thomas Wriothesley, first Earl of Southampton, announced Henry's death to Parliament. Edward was proclaimed King Edward VI. He arrived in London that afternoon.

February. Edward VI was crowned by Archbishop Cranmer who used the occasion to assert the divine right of kings.

March 5. Thomas Wriothesley was removed from the Council because he had acted without consent of the Council in appointing deputies.

May. Edward Seymour was secretly wed to Catherine Parr.

September 10. The Battle of Pinkie in Scotland was fought. It was the last and bloodiest battle between the two kingdoms.

1548

March 8. The new Order of Communion forbade the priest to vary old rites and ceremonies of the mass.

September. Catherine Parr died.

1549   March 30. Lord High Admiral Thomas Seymour was beheaded on Tower Hill.

June 1. Protector Somerset issued a proclamation against enclosures and appointed a commission to make a return of enclosures.

June 9. Whit-Sunday was the date on which every Parish priest was to adopt the Book of Common Prayer.

July. William Kett's rebellion occurred because of enclosures.

August 8. The Anglo-French War began.

September. Edmund, Bishop of London, was sent to the Tower for resisting the new Service. A Cabal was formed against the Protector.

October 10. Somerset was arrested after having fled to London when he could not get the Commons to rise on his and the King's behalf. He was sent to the Tower on October 14.

1550   February 6. Somerset was released from the Tower because his prosecution could not be connected with attacks on the Catholics.

March 29. Peace with France was proclaimed in London.

1551   February 14. Bishop Gardiner was sentenced to deprivation. His appeal to the King was rejected.

June. The coinage was debased.

October 11. Many men were given titles, including John Dudley, Earl of Warwick, who was created Duke of Northumberland.

October 16. Somerset was sent to the Tower again. He was charged with plotting to assassinate members of the Council.

December 1. Somerset's trial began. He was convicted and sentenced to death. He was executed January 22, 1552.

1552

January. Parliament reassembled and passed the Second Act of Uniformity.

October. A Commission was appointed to examine heresies.

1553

June. Cranmer's Forty-Two Articles were published with a Catechism by Bishop Poncet.

July 6. Edward VI died.

July 10. Lady Jane Grey was declared Queen.

July 19. The Council declared for Mary.

August 3. Mary entered London.

August 13. The Protestants rose against Catholic developments.

August 18. Northumberland was tried and convicted of treason for having supported the cause of Lady Jane Grey. He was executed August 22.

August - September. Archbishop Cranmer, as well as Latimer and others, was arrested.

October. Parliament repealed the treason laws and Edward VI's ecclesiastical legislation.

October 30. Mary proposed her marriage with King Philip of Spain.

1554

February 12. Lady Jane Grey was executed.

February 23. Elizabeth arrived at Westminster. She was sent to the Tower on March 18.

May 19. Elizabeth was released from the Tower and sent to Woodstock.

July 25. Mary and Philip were married.

November. Mary became convinced that she was pregnant. The pretext was kept up until August 1555.

November 29. Both Houses of Parliament passed a petition for reunion with Rome.

November 30. England was absolved of the sins of heresy of the Reformation.

December 12. The House of Commons reenacted the heresy laws.

1555   January 16. The House of Commons passed a proposal to make it treason to "pray or desire" that God shorten the Queen's days.

December 18. Persecution of the Protestants was renewed.

1556   March 21. Cranmer was executed.

1557   June 7. England declared war on France.

1558   November 17. Mary and Cardinal Pole both died within a few hours of each other.

November 18. Elizabeth was declared Queen.

December 30. English was introduced into the Church service.

1559   January 13. Elizabeth was crowned.

March. England concluded peace with Scotland.

March 22. Parliament passed the Act of Supremacy.

March 24. Elizabeth refused to agree to the Supremacy bill.

April 2. Peace Treaty of Cateau-Cambresis was concluded with France.

April 29. New Act of Supremacy was passed.

1560   January. The Elizabethan settlement of religion was
            achieved in Ireland.

            July 6. Treaty of Edinburgh was signed between Scots,
            English and France.

            December 5. Francis II of France died. His widow was
            Mary Queen of Scots. Mary returned to Scotland, August
            1561.

1562   September 22. The Treaty of Hampton Court was signed by
            Elizabeth with Prince of Condé's agent. Elizabeth was to
            assist the Huguenots with men and money and to hold
            Havre until Calais was restored.

            October. John Hawkins made his first voyage to the new
            world. He made his second trip in 1564-65.

1564   April 11. The Treaty of Troyes arranged for peace between
            England and France.

1565   July 29. Lord Darnley married Mary Queen of Scots.

1566   March 9. David Rizzio, Mary Queen of Scots Secretary
            and favorite, was murdered practically in Mary's pre-
            sence. She swore vengeance.

            June 19. The future James VI was born.

1567   February 10. Darnley was murdered while recuperating
            at his home, which was blown up. The Earl of Bothwell
            was involved.

            May 15. Mary Queen of Scots married Bothwell after the
            latter was divorced from his wife.

            June 15. The Scottish nobles allied against Mary Stuart
            and captured her at Carberry Hill.

            July 16. Mary was forced to abdicate in favor of her son,
            James, with the Earl of Moray as Regent in Scotland.

1568   May 2. Mary Stuart escaped from Loch Leven, repudiat-
            ed her abdication and joined the Hamiltons against the
            Regent.

May 16. Mary's forces were defeated and she fled to England.

October. Hawkins made his third voyage to the new world.

October 3. Elizabeth's Commissioners Norfolk, Sussex, and Sir Ralph Sadler met Mary's representatives Leslie, Bishop of Ross and Lord Herries at York.

December. The English seized Spanish treasure ships. Philip of Spain expelled Elizabeth's ambassador.

1569   September 30. After fleeing from Elizabeth because of his plans to marry Mary, Norfolk surrendered. He was committed to the Tower on October 11.

October 24. The Northern nobles rose in rebellion.

1570   February 25. Elizabeth was ex-communicated by Pope Pius V.

1572   April 21. Treaty of Blois, defensive alliance between England and France, was signed.

May 8. Elizabeth called Parliament into session ostensibly to deal with religious issues but actually to push for the execution of Norfolk.

August 22. Norfolk and Northumberland were executed.

August 24. The Massacre of St. Bartholomew occurred in France. Many Protestants were killed. The English reacted to this.

1574   August 28. Convention of Bristol was signed settling differences between England and Spain over seizure of Spanish treasure ships.

1578   March 12. James VI assumed the reins of government in Scotland.

1579   August. The Duke of Anjou visited Elizabeth in England.

1580   March. Negotiations for Elizabeth's marriage with Anjou were revived.

June 25. Edmund Campion, a priest, landed in England.
He was arrested at Lyford, July 16, 1581. He was con-
demned after torture and executed December 1.

1581   January. Parliament met and passed an act requiring
            obedience of the Queen's subjects to the Anglican Church.

1583   October. Francis Throckmorton was seized when writing a
            letter in cipher to Mary Stuart to help her gain the throne.

1585   July 31. Anglo-Scottish agreement for a defensive alli-
            ance was signed to counter the arrangements of the
            Catholic League.

            August 12. A treaty was signed between England and the
            Netherlands. Elizabeth was to supply men and arms to
            the Dutch.

1586   October 11. Mary Stuart was tried and convicted for con-
            spiracy in Babington plot to assassinate Elizabeth and
            place Mary on the throne of England.

            November 12. Both Houses of Parliament petitioned for
            Mary Stuart's death.

1587   Christopher Marlowe wrote Tamburlaine.

            February 1. Elizabeth signed the death-warrant for
            Mary Stuart. She was executed on February 8.

            April 19. Sir Francis Drake appeared before Cadiz and
            sank or burned 33 vessels. Then he seized Sagres.

1588   Christopher Marlowe wrote Dr. Faustus.

            July. Spanish Armada set sail. It was in sight of Eng-
            land on July 19.

            July 21-25. Spanish and English fleets fought in the
            English Channel.

            July 29. Battle of Gravelines was fought. It was an
            English victory. The Armada was dispersed between
            August and September.

1590	William Shakespeare's <u>Comedy</u> <u>of</u> <u>Errors</u> appeared.
1591	Shakespeare produced <u>Two</u> <u>Gentlemen</u> <u>of</u> <u>Verona</u>.
	August 2. Sir Robert Cecil was admitted to the Privy Council as Secretary.
1592	Trinity College, Dublin, was founded.
	Shakespeare wrote the three parts of <u>Henry</u> <u>VI</u>.
1593	William Shakespeare's <u>Venus</u> <u>and</u> <u>Adonis</u>, as well as his <u>Richard</u> <u>III</u>, appeared.
1595	About this time, William Shakespeare wrote the following: <u>Romeo</u> <u>and</u> <u>Juliet,</u> <u>Midsummer</u> <u>Night's</u> <u>Dream</u> and <u>Merchant</u> <u>of</u> <u>Venice</u>.
1596	January 27. Sir Francis Drake died on his last voyage off Puerto Rico.
	Between 1596 and 1599, Shakespeare wrote <u>Henry</u> <u>IV</u> and <u>Henry</u> <u>V</u>, as well as <u>The</u> <u>Merry</u> <u>Wives</u> <u>of</u> <u>Windsor</u>.
1598	August 4. William Cecil, Lord Burghley, died.
1599	Between 1599 and 1601, Shakespeare wrote <u>As</u> <u>You</u> <u>Like</u> <u>It,</u> <u>All's</u> <u>Well</u> <u>That</u> <u>Ends</u> <u>Well</u>, <u>Much</u> <u>Ado</u> <u>About</u> <u>Nothing</u> and <u>Twelfth</u> <u>Night</u>.
1600	April. William Adams landed in Japan and proceeded to build the Japanese navy.
	December 31. The East India Company was chartered.
1601	Shakespeare produced <u>Julius</u> <u>Caesar</u> and <u>Hamlet</u> between 1601 and 1603.
	November 20. Elizabeth made her final address to Parliament.
1603	March 24. <u>Elizabeth died.</u> She was succeeded by James I.

THE SEVENTEENTH CENTURY

STUARTS - CIVIL WAR AND COMMONWEALTH - RESTORATION

1603

Between 1603 and 1609, Shakespeare produced Troilus and Cressida, Measure for Measure, Othello, Macbeth, King Lear, Timon of Athens and Anthony and Cleopatra.

June 24. This day was chosen for Bye Plot, whereby Roman Catholic Priest conspired with others to seize James and demand that he be lenient with Catholics. The plot was uncovered.

November 17. Sir Walter Raleigh was tried because of suspicion of his part in plot to dethrone the King. He was found guilty of high treason and sentenced to death.

1604

January 14. Hampton Court Conference was held. The Puritans demanded reforms in the Church. James permitted a few minor changes but would not eliminate the hierarchy.

August 19. A Peace Treaty was signed between England and Spain.

1605

November 4. Gunpowder Plot was discovered in which plans were made to kill the Cabinet. Guy Fawkes was arrested.

1606

April 10. James I granted a charter for the colony of Virginia.

1607

April 26. Three ships of the London Company arrived at the mouth of the Chesapeake Bay. The colony of Jamestown was eventually founded.

May. The settlement on the Kennebac River was founded.

1609

Shakespeare wrote Coriolanus, followed by Cymbeline, Winter's Tale and The Tempest in the next few years.

1612

November 5. Henry, Prince of Wales, died at the age of 18.

1613	February 14. Lady Elizabeth, daughter of James I, married the Elector Palatine.
1614	August. George Villiers was introduced to King James.
1617	January 5. George Villiers was created Earl of Buckingham.
	June 12. Walter Raleigh sailed for South America. His mission was a failure.
1618	January 7. Francis Bacon became Lord Chancellor.
	October 29. Sir Walter Raleigh was executed. He had never been pardoned after being convicted of treason in 1604.
1619	August 26. Frederick, Elector of Palatine, was elected King of Bohemia.
	October 29. The Battle of White Mountain was fought, Frederick's cause to gain the Empire was defeated.
1620	September 6. Group of Pilgrims set sail for America from Plymouth on board Mayflower. They sighted Cape Cod on November 9. They landed December 11 on the shores of Plymouth Bay, having already drawn up an instrument of government.
1621	May 3. Francis Bacon was convicted of corruption by Lords.
1623	February 17. Charles, Prince of Wales, and the Duke of Buckingham went to Spain to arrange the Marriage Treaty with the Infanta.
	October 5. Charles and Buckingham landed at Portsmouth. James I was soon disappointed to learn that the marriage would not go through.
1624	November 10. The French marriage treaty was signed by ambassadors. It was ratified by James I on December 12.
1625	March 27. James I died. His son, Charles I, succeeded to the throne.

June 13. Charles I married Henrietta Maria of France.

October 8. Fleet sailed for Cadiz. It failed to defeat the Spanish.

1628   June 7. Charles I assented to the Petition of Right which restrained the King from exacting any gift, loan, benevolence or tax; forbade the imprisonment of any man without cause requiring the writ of <u>habeas</u> <u>corpus</u>.

1629   March 10. Parliament was dissolved after continuous rankling with the King. Sir John Eliot and others were arrested.

April 14. A Peace Treaty with France was signed.

1630   November 5. Francis Cottington signed the Treaty of Peace between England and Spain.

1634   October. First writ of ship-money was issued to raise money for the Crown without going to Parliament.

1635   August 4. Second writ of ship money was issued, extending it from the sea coast towns to the whole country.

1636   October 9. Third writ of ship money was issued. Two private men undertook to make the only possible protest against the ship money by refusing to pay, thus compelling the case to be argued in a court of law. Lord Saye, the staunchest Puritan among the peers, and the other, John Hampden, wealthy squire of Buckingham, forced the issue. The majority of judges ruled in the King's favor.

1639   June 18. Charles I and the Scots signed the Treaty of Berwick by which both sides agreed to disband their armies, but it left the gravest difference between the King and the Scots undetermined.

1640   April 13. The English Parliament met with the request to grant the King money. Henry Vane thought that Charles might be able to get twelve subsidies or Ł840,000 to fight the Scots.

May 4. Vane asked Parliament for 12 subsidies in return for abandonment of the claim to ship money.

May 5. As a result of the opposition by Parliament, it was dissolved.

August 20. The Scots invaded England.

September 24. A great assembly of nobles met at York to assist Charles in his movements, perhaps even with their wealth. 16 peers were chosen to meet with the Scots.

October 2. The Peers met with the Scottish representatives at Ripon.

October 21. Treaty of Ripon was signed by which the King's representatives agreed to pay the Scots ₤850 per day or about ₤25,000 a month while they occupied the northern counties in return for a cessation of fighting.

November 3. The Long Parliament assembled.

November 25. The House of Commons impeached Strafford, who was committed to the Tower on the same day.

December 18. The Lords sequestered Archbishop Laud and committed him to James Maxwell's custody.

1641

February 16. Charles accepted the Triennial Act. The purpose was to ensure that there never be more than a three year interval between two sessions of Parliament.

March 22. Trial of Strafford began. The charges against him were in reality against Charles I because Strafford had only tried to increase the King's power.

May 12. Strafford was executed.

August 10. Charles I went to Scotland.

September 9. The two Houses of Parliament adjourned. They reassembled on October 20.

November 23. The Grand Remonstrance was passed. It was a statement of all that had gone wrong since the accession of Charles, as well as a statement of all reforms made by the Parliament then sitting, and finally a summary of the reforms still needed to perfect the work.

November 25. Charles I returned to London.

1642

January 3. Charles ordered the Attorney-General, Sir Edward Herbert, to prepare articles of impeachment against five members of the House of Commons: John Pym, John Hampden, Denzil Holles, Sir Arthur Hazle-rigg and William Strode in order to save the Queen from impeachment.

January 4. Charles visited the House of Commons, only to find that the accused had left. Parliament was angered by his actions.

February 23. Queen Henrietta Maria sailed from Dover with the crown jewels to raise a large sum of cash for the defense of the monarchy.

June 1. Parliament despatched the famous Nineteen Propositions to the King, basically intended to mean that the Parliament and not the King was to be the sovereign of England.

August 22. Charles I raised his standard at Nottingham. The Civil War thus began.

October 23. The Houses of Parliament won the Battle of Edgehill.

1643

February 1. The Parliamentary Commissioners opened negotiations with the King which led to the Treaty of Oxford.

September 25. The Solemn League and Covenant was signed to abolish the episcopacy in London; maintain the privileges and liberties of England and Scotland; to preserve the King's authority; and to bring incendiaries and malignants to justice.

December 8. John Pym died.

1644

July 2. The Parliamentary army defeated the Royalists at the Battle of Marston Moor.

December 19. The Self-Denying Ordinance was passed, which moved the exclusion of members of either House from all office or command, civil or military, during the war. The House of Lords attacked it.

1645   January 4. The ordinance of attainder for Archbishop Laud was passed. Laud was executed on January 10.

June 14. The Battle of Naseby was fought in which Charles suffered a complete defeat.

1646   April 26. Charles went to the Scottish army. He was taken prisoner by the Scots on May 5.

1647   February 3. Charles was delivered to Parliament when the Scots were paid Ŀ200,000, one-half of the sum to be paid to cover the costs of their army.

June 15. The Council of the Army issued the Declaration of the Army, requiring that Commons be purged of offending members and that the date for its dissolution be fixed; that future Parliaments be limited as to their existence; that the right of petition be recognized; that offenses be punished according to law, not at the discretion of the Houses; that national accounts be published; and in most cases that amnesty be granted.

November 11. Charles fled from Hampton Court.

December 26. Charles signed the Engagement Treaty with the Scots. He would confirm the Presbyterian establishment for three years if he and Parliament could regulate the Church.

1648   September 18. Negotiations between the King and Parliament began at Newport. They lasted 40 days.

December 2. The army occupied London.

December 6. Pride's Purge occurred by which Colonel Pride turned out all obnoxious members of Parliament. Only the Rump remained. Cromwell approved of the action.

1649   January 6. The Commons passed an act, erecting a high court of justice for the King's trial.

January 19. The trial of Charles I opened. He was sentenced to death on January 27.

January 30. Charles was executed.

May 19. An act was passed, declaring England a free Commonwealth.

September 11. Oliver Cromwell stormed Drogheda in Ireland. He ordered the slaughter of everyone captured to set an example.

1650   May 1. Charles II agreed to the Scottish terms in the Treaty of Breda. He was to take the covenant and void all treaties with the Irish.

December 24. Edinburgh Castle surrendered, and the English became masters of all southern Scotland.

1651   September 3. Charles and his forces were defeated at the Battle of Worcester by Cromwell and his troops.

October. Parliament passed the Navigation Act, whereby goods from other continents had to be imported in English ships, or with a crew that was one-half English. Goods from a European country were to be imported in an English ship or a ship of the country of origin. It was aimed against the Dutch carrying trade.

October 16. Charles escaped to France.

October 27. Articles of Capitulation were signed at Limerick by the Irish.

1652   August 2. The army officers adopted a petition, demanding maintenance other than tithes for ministers, reform of the law, better financial administration, provision of work for the poor, payment of arrears to troops and election of a new representative body.

1653   April 20. Cromwell expelled Parliament.

July 4. The Little Parliament, especially called by Cromwell, met at Whitehall. It was criticized in the long run for failing to fulfill all its promises. This marks the highest point of the Puritan Revolution. It ended December 12.

December 16. Cromwell was inaugurated as Protector under a new Instrument of Government.

1654   April 5. A Treaty of Peace was signed with the Dutch in which the latter recognized British mastery of the seas.

July 10. Treaty with Portugal was signed whereby the English were permitted to trade in Portugal and all its possessions.

December. West Indies' expedition was sent out under Admiral William Penn and General Robert Venables.

1655   May 11. Jamaica was conquered.

October. The Major-Generals received their commissions to govern.

October 24. An Anglo-French Treaty of Friendship was signed.

1656   April 2. A treaty was concluded in Brussels between Charles II and Philip of Spain. The latter was to supply Charles with troops in return for which Charles would aid Philip in reconquering Portugal.

September 9. The Spanish Plate fleet was destroyed.

1657   May 25. Cromwell accepted an amended Petition and Advice with the offer of a Crown omitted.

1658   June 4. The Battle of the Dunes was fought in which the English defeated the Spaniards.

September 3. Oliver Cromwell died. He was succeeded by his son, Richard, as Lord Protector.

1659   April 19. Richard Cromwell declared the Council of Officers dissolved.

May 7. The Long Parliament was restored. Richard soon retired to Hampton Court and then into obscurity until his death in 1712.

October 12. The second expulsion of the Long Parliament was carried out by John Lambert.

December 26. The Army restored the Long Parliament.

1660 February 3. General Monk and his troops marched into London.

March 16. Parliament dissolved itself.

March. Charles II issued the Declaration of Breda, promising indemnity to all offenders not excepted from the pardon by Parliament, agreeing to an act of liberty of consciences, as well as the validity of sales of land during the revolution and payment of arrears to soldiers.

April 25. The Convention Parliament met.

May 8. Charles was proclaimed King. He entered London May 29.

August 29. The Act of Indemnity and Oblivion was passed, excepting only a few regicides and other supporters of the Revolution.

1661 January 30. The bodies of Cromwell, Ireton and Bradshaw were hung at Tyburn and buried beneath the gallows.

September 27. The Irish Act of Settlement was passed declaring that all lands forfeited since November 23, 1641, were to be returned.

1662 May 27. The Scottish Parliament restored all privileges and powers of the Bishops.

December 26. Charles II issued the first Declaration of Indulgence, asking Parliament for the power to dispense with the acts that he thought necessary.

1665 February 22. England declared war against the Dutch.

1666 September 2-6. Great fire of London occurred, which destroyed two-thirds of the capital.

1667 Milton's Paradise Lost was published.

July 21. Peace of Breda was signed with the Dutch. England annexed New York and New Jersey.

1668   January 23. Convention of the Hague was signed by the United Netherlands and England.

May 2. Louis XIV made peace with Spain at Aix-la-Chapelle.

1670   May 22. The Secret Treaty of Dover was signed whereby Charles was to declare himself a Catholic, Louis to supply money and men, England to aid France against Spain and the two states (England and France) were to attack the United Netherlands.

1671   Milton's <u>Paradise Regained</u> and <u>Samson Agonistes</u> appeared.

The Sham Treaty was signed with France to dupe the Duke of Buckingham and his colleagues.

1672   March 17. The Second Dutch War broke out.

1673   March 29. The Test Act was passed, requiring that an individual had to take the Anglican sacrament in order to take office.

June. The Duke of York refused to take the test and resigned his office.

November 21. James married his second wife, Mary of Modena, a Catholic.

1674   February 9. The Treaty of Westminster was signed between England and Spain, granting favorable terms to the Dutch.

1676   James openly avowed his change of faith.

1677   November 4. William of Orange married Mary, James' eldest daughter.

1678   September 28. Titus Oates and Dr. Israel Tonge appeared before the Privy Council with their story of the Popish plot that the Jesuits planned to kill Charles II. Oates accused the Queen of high treason in plotting to kill Charles on November 28. The Lords would not go along, and this last preposterous charge was removed.

1680   June 10. England and Spain concluded a treaty agreeing to
                maintain the Peace of Nimwegen.

1681   March 14. Charles made a secret agreement with France.
                Charles was to receive a subsidy for three years in return
                for ending England's alliance with Spain.

                December. The Writ of Quo Warranto was issued against
                London in order to challenge its liberties.

1683   February. Robert Ferguson, associate of Shaftesbury,
                returned to England and formed Rye House Plot to seize
                Charles and James in April.

                July 21. Convocation of Oxford University issued a de-
                cree condemning all works and people who challenged the
                Anglican Church.

                July. James' second daughter, Anne, married Prince
                George of Denmark.

1685   February 6. Charles II died. He was succeeded by
                James II.

                May 19. The Tory Parliament met, indicating its sup-
                port for James.

                June 11. The Duke of Monmouth, Charles II's illegitimate
                son, raised forces against James. He was defeated and
                captured. He was executed July 15.

1687   Sir Isaac Newton published his Principia Mathematica.

                April. John Dryden published The Hind and the Panther.

                April 4. The Declaration of Indulgence was issued,
                granting freedom of worship to all recusants, Catholic
                or Protestant.

1688   April 27. The Second Declaration of Indulgence was
                issued.

                June 10. A son was born to James and his Queen.

September 2. James announced his consent to the permanent exclusion of Papists from the House of Commons.

October 22. James summoned an extraordinary council to give proof of the birth of the Prince of Wales.

THE GLORIOUS REVOLUTION AND AFTER

November 5. William of Orange landed at Torbay. He came at the invitation of Parliament which was disturbed with the idea of a Catholic dynasty.

December 9. James went to Faversham near the Thames where he left for France.

December 11. Faversham fishermen boarded James' ship in the process of priest-hunting. They took James and his companions prisoners.

December 15. James made a formal entry into London.

December 17. James left Whitehall for the last time. William entered London that evening.

1689   February 12. The Declaration of Right was completed. Mary arrived from Holland.

February 13. William III and Mary II were proclaimed King and Queen.

March 24. James entered Dublin in state.

April 12. The coronation of William and Mary took place.

December 16. The Bill of Rights received the Royal assent.

1690   July 1. The Battle of the Boyne was won by the English under William III. William entered Dublin on July 6.

1692   May 19. The Battle of La Hogue was fought. It was the last great naval engagement of the War and put an end to projected invasion of England by the French.

October 30. William returned to England. He was angered over Mary's handling of the naval administration.

1693	William Congreve became famous with The Old Bachelor.
1694	April 25. The Bank of England was founded.

December 22. William accepted the Triennial Act, guaranteeing that Parliament would be elected every three years.

December 28. Mary II died.

1696   January 21. The recoinage Act received the royal assent. William also agreed to the bill to regulate trials for treason in which two witnesses were required.

1697   November 2. The Treaty of Ryswick was completed. It led to resumption of relations between England and France.

1700   March 14. The Second Partition Treaty was signed, dividing the Spanish possessions after the death of the King. The Dutch signed on March 15.

October 3. The dying King of Spain, Charles II, bequeathed the succession to Philip of Anjou, second son of the Dauphin of France. If the latter inherited the French' throne, his younger brother, the Duke of Berry, was to be the Spanish King. Charles died on November 1. Louis XIV accepted the will. Emperor Leopold was opposed. He needed the aid of England and the Netherlands.

1701   June 12. The Act of Settlement was passed, recognizing the Electress Sophia and her heirs, being Protestant, as successors after Anne and any descendants of Anne or William.

September 6. James II died at St. Germain. Louis XIV had already decided to recognize young James Edward as his father's successor.

September 7. The Grand Alliance was signed at the Hague by England, the German Empire and the Netherlands.

December 24. The two East India Companies were merged.

1702	March 8. William III died. He was succeeded by Anne.
	March 12. First daily newspaper, The Daily Courant, appeared.
	April 23. Anne was crowned Queen of England.
	May 4. England declared war against France and Spain.
	December 16-27. John Methuen concluded the Methuen Treaty which gave England a monopoly for her woolen goods in Portugese markets, granting preferential duties to Portugese wines.
1704	February 17. The first number of Daniel Defoe's Review appeared. It ceased June 1717.
	August 6. Admiral Sir George Rooke captured Gibraltar.
	August 13. Marlborough was victorious at the Battle of Blenheim.
1706	May 12. Marlborough won the victory of Ramillies.
	December 3. The Whigs were removed from office and the Whigs, including Sunderland as Secretary of State, were appointed.
1707	January 16. The Treaty for Union of England and Scotland was approved by Queen Anne.
1708	July 11. Marlborough won the victory of Oudenarde against the French.
	October 28. Prince George of Denmark, husband of Anne, died.
	November 22. Marlborough relieved Brussels.
1709	April 12. First number of Richard Steele's Tatler appeared. It stopped publication January 2, 1711.
	September 11. Marlborough won the victory of Malplaquet.

1710   January. Friction developed between Marlborough and
                         the Queen.

                         February 27. The trial of Rev. Henry Sacheverell
                         opened. He was accused of preaching sermons against
                         latitudinarianism and the Church. He was sentenced on
                         March 23. He was not permitted to preach for three
                         years, and his offending sermons were ordered burned.

                         April 6. Queen Anne and the Duchess of Marlborough
                         had their final falling out.

1711   January 17. The Duchess of Marlborough was dismissed
                         from office.

                         March 1. The Spectator appeared. Joseph Addison wrote
                         a total of 274 and Richard Steele, 236.

                         December 31. Marlborough was removed from office
                         because of bitterness of the ministry toward him.

1712   Alexander Pope wrote The Rape of the Lock.

1713   March. The Guardian appeared.

1714   April 11. The Treaty of Peace was signed at Utrecht.

                         August 1. Queen Anne died. George I succeeded her to
                         the throne.

                         THE GEORGIAN ERA: 1714 - 1837

                         August 6. George I signed a commission naming Marl-
                         borough Captain-General.

                         September 18. George I arrived at Greenwich.

1715   September 6. The Earl of Mar proclaimed the Pre-
                         tender King.

                         November 1. Scottish rebels entered England.

                         December 22. The Pretender James landed at Peterhead,
                         Scotland.

1716   February 4. James left for France.

February 6. The Treaty of Westminster between England and the States General was signed. It was the beginning of the Quadruple Alliance.

May 7. George I approved of the Septennial Act, whereby Parliament was to last seven years.

July 7. George I left for Hanover. He left his son as regent.

1717   January 4. The Triple Alliance was concluded between England, France and Holland.

January 18. George I returned to London.

1718   August 2. A treaty was signed in London by the representatives of Great Britain, France and the Empire. It became the Quadruple Alliance in December when the Dutch adhered to it.

August 11. Sir George Byng destroyed the Spanish fleet off Cape Passaro.

1720   April 7. The South Sea Act received the royal assent. It provided for paying off the national debt by incorporating it with the stock for the South Sea Company. The bubble burst, however, during the autumn when the price fell because it had been highly inflated. Parliament investigated the company.

December 31. Charles Edward, the young Pretender, was born.

1721   June 13. A defensive alliance was signed by England, France and Spain.

1724   April. Jonathan Swift's first "Drapier's Letter" was published, criticizing William Wood's new coinage for Ireland. Several others were written during the course of the year. The British government yielded on the issue of the new coinage on August 26.

1725   September 3. The Treaty of Hanover, a defensive, alli-
ance, was signed by Great Britain, France and Prussia.
The latter defected from the Treaty on October 12, 1726.
Sweden adhered to it on March 26, 1727.

1727   May 31. Austria signed preliminary Peace Treaty of
Paris with England, France and Holland.

June 11. George I died. He was succeeded by George II.

1728   John Gay's Beggars' Opera appeared.

1729   November 9. Treaty of Seville between England, Spain,
and France was signed.

1730   Matthew Tindal's Christianity as Old as the Creation
appeared advocating Deism.

May 15. Viscount Charles Townshend resigned from
the Cabinet. He became an agricultural reformer and
was known as "Turnip Townshend."

1733   Alexander Pope wrote his Essay on Man, completing it
in 1734.

November 7. Family compact between Spain and France
was signed.

1736   April 27. Frederick, Prince of Wales, married Princess Augusta, daughter of Frederick, Duke of Saxe-
Gotha.

1737   November 20. Queen Caroline died.

1739   October 19. War was declared against Spain.

1742   November 18. Treaty with Russia was signed at Westminster by which each sovereign guaranteed the other's
territories and protected Hanover against a French raid.

1744   March 4. Louis XV declared war against England.

March 29. English counter-declaration of war was announced.

June 27. Commodore Peter Warren captured Louisbourg in North America.

1745   August 19. Prince Charles Edward, the Pretender, appeared with an army in Scotland.

September 17. The Jacobite army occupied Edinburgh.

December 20. Prince Charles recrossed the border after making a foray into England. He was eventually defeated during 1746.

1747   May 3. Admiral Anson defeated the French off Cape Finisterre.

1748   Tobias Smollet's earliest novel, Roderick Random, appeared.

April 19. Peace of Aix-la-Chapelle was concluded. France and England agreed to reciprocally restore their conquests.

1750   October 30. Treaty of Madrid was signed. Great Britain surrendered the South Sea Company's Assiento rights.

1751   March 20. Frederick, Prince of Wales, died.

1753   July 7. Hardwicke's Marriage Act was passed, declaring that all marriages which were celebrated irregularly, without proper advance announcement, were void.

July 7. The Jews were naturalized.

1755   July 9. General Braddock was defeated by the French and their Indian allies near Fort Duquesne.

1756   January 16. The Convention of Westminster was signed whereby Prussia and England agreed to unite to resist invasion of Germany by foreign powers.

June 20. The Nawab of Bengal attacked Calcutta, capturing 146 Englishmen. They were put into the Black Hole of Calcutta from which only 23 survived.

November. Pitt formed a ministry to wage war.

1757   April 6. Pitt was dismissed, but he eventually returned
            to office when he was needed to continue the war.

            June 23. Robert Clive defeated the French at Plassy in
            India.

1758   July 26. Louisbourg was captured.

1759   September 18. General James Wolfe captured Quebec,
            but he died of wounds received in battle.

1760   September 8. Montreal capitulated to General Jeffrey
            Amherst.

            October 25. George II died. He was succeeded by his
            grandson, George III.

1761   September 8. George III married Princess Charlotte,
            daughter of the Duke of Mecklenberg-Strelitz.

            October 5. Pitt resigned from office.

1762   January 4. War was declared against Spain.

1763   February 10. The definitive peace of Paris was signed.
            England gained Canada.

            April 23. North Briton Number 45 appeared, denouncing
            George III's speech proroguing Parliament. General
            warrant was issued ordering the arrest of the authors,
            printers and publishers. 49 persons were arrested.

1764   January 19. The House of Commons expelled John Wilkes,
            author of the North Briton.

1765   March 23. The Stamp Act was passed, leading to resis-
            tance in the American colonies and a challenge to the
            right of taxation.

1766   Edward Gibbon published the first volume of his Decline
            and Fall of the Roman Empire. The last volume was
            published in 1788.

            March 11. The Stamp Act was repealed. The Declaratory
            Act was passed at the same time, indicating the right of
            Britain to tax the colonies.

1767   June. A bill was passed based on an agreement with the
East India Company, which in return for confirmation of
its territorial revenues, bound itself to pay the government Ь400,000 a year for two years. Parliament prohibited a higher dividend than 10%. The agreement was renewed in 1769.

      November 20. Two acts were passed affecting the colo-
nies, one providing for the execution of the trade laws,
and the other imposing duties on the importation of glass,
paper, paints and tea.

1769   February 3. The Commons voted to expel Wilkes after
he published Viscount Weymouth's letter to London magistrates suggesting that they call in the military, if
necessary. Wilkes was reelected by the Middlesex voters
on February 16. The House annulled the election of
February 17. Wilkes was returned again on March 16,
and the election was annulled again.

      April 13. In a new election, Wilkes defeated Colonel
Luttrell, but the House voted on April 15 that Luttrell
ought to have been returned.

1770   January 28. Lord North formed a new administration.

      March 3. The Boston massacre occurred when the troops
fired on a mob who had been abusing a sentinel and then
turned on the troops.

1773   May. Robert Clive, accused of misconduct in India, was
acquitted.

      June. Lord North's Regulating Bill was passed, limiting
the authority of the East India Company in India.

      December 16. The Boston Tea Party was held to protest
the tea tax.

1774   September 5. The first meeting of the Continental Congress was held in Philadelphia with only Georgia unrepre-
sented.

1775   April 19. Fighting occurred at Lexington and Concord,
Massachusetts.

May. The Americans seized Ticonderoga and Crown Point.

June 15. George Washington was appointed American Commander-in-Chief.

June 17. Battle of Bunker Hill was fought. The British victory enabled them to hold Boston for nine months longer.

1776   Adam Smith's Nature and the Causes of the Wealth of Nations appeared.

July 4. The Americans issued the Declaration of Independence.

1778   February 6. An alliance was concluded between France and the Americans.

1780   June 2-7. Lord George Gordon riots occurred against any emancipation for Catholics.

December 2. War was declared against the Dutch.

1781   October 19. Lord Cornwallis surrendered to the Americans at Yorktown.

1782   November 30. The Americans signed the preliminaries of peace without consulting the French.

1783   September 3. The final Peace Treaty of Versailles was signed.

December 19. George III demanded the resignation of the Coalition Ministry. William Pitt, the younger, became Prime Minister at the age of 25.

1784   August 13. Pitt's Government of India Bill was passed. It subordinated the political power exercised by the directors to the board of control.

1786   September 26. A Commercial Treaty was signed with France, the Eden Treaty, reducing duties on many of the principal articles of commerce of both countries.

1788   February 13. The trial of Warren Hastings began for high crimes and misdemeanors in his administration of India. He was acquitted in 1795.

April. Triple Alliance of Great Britain, Prussia and the United Provinces was signed, providing for mutual defense and peace.

1789   October 28. Treaty between Britain and Spain was signed recognizing British demands for trading in Nootka Sound.

1790   November. Edmund Burke published his Reflections on the French Revolution, attacking the state of affairs in France.

1791   May. Rupture occurred between Burke and Charles James Fox over the issue of the French Revolution which Fox supported.

1792   May 21. The Government issued a proclamation against seditious writings.

1793   February 1. France declared war on England.

March 15. Traitorous correspondence bill was enacted.

1795   April 8. George, Prince of Wales, married Caroline, daughter of the Duke of Brunswick. Prince George agreed only because Parliament had promised to pay his debts.

The Speenhamland magistrates decided upon a system of supplementing low wages to cover the cost of bread and rents through the dole.

May 4. The Government agreed to guarantee a loan of £4,600,000 to enable the Austrian Emperor to raise an army of 200,000 men. Then they concluded defensive treaties with Russia and Austria.

1797   February 14. The British defeated the Spaniards at the Battle of Cape St. Vincent.

February 27. The Bank of England suspended cash payments.

October 11. Admiral Duncan led the British and Dutch
fleets in defeating the French at the Battle of Camperdown.

November. The government assessed triple taxes.

1798   Malthus first published an Essay on Population anony-
mously.

William Wordsworth and Samuel Taylor Coleridge published Lyrical Ballads including the latter's "Rhyme of
the Ancient Mariner".

November 1. The Battle of the Nile was fought in which
Admiral Horatio Nelson defeated the French fleet, leaving Napoleon Bonaparte's troops isolated in France.

December-January 1799. The Second Coalition was
formed, including Russia, Naples, Great Britain and
Prussia.

1799   December 25. Napoleon sent a letter to George III, asking for peace.

1800   June 20. Sir Gilbert Elliot, the Earl of Minto, signed a
convention with Austria which guaranteed a loan to the
Emperor.

August 1. The Union between Ireland and Great Britain
was enacted.

December 16. The League of Armed Neutrality was
formed by Russia, Sweden and Denmark against Britain.

1801   January. George III made known his opposition to Catholic Emancipation proposed in September 1800 by Pitt.
Pitt indicated that he would resign if it were not granted.

February 20. King George III became insane again. Pitt
promised in March when the King's health improved that
he would not bother him again on the issue of Catholic
emancipation.

March 14. Pitt resigned his office.

March 21. French Army was defeated at the Battle of
Alexandria by the British under Sir Ralph Abercrombie.
The French evacuated Egypt in September.

1802   William Cobbett's <u>Weekly</u> <u>Political</u> <u>Register</u> was first
published.

The <u>Edinburgh</u> <u>Review</u> was founded.

March 27. Great Britain, France, Spain and the Batavian
Republic signed the Peace of Amiens.

November. Col. Edward M. Despard was arrested because he and 36 followers plotted to kill the King and
seize government buildings to establish the constitutional
independence of Ireland and Great Britain. Despard was
found guilty of high treason and was executed on February 21, 1803.

1803   May 18. War with France was renewed.

1804   July. The Third Coalition was formed by Great Britain,
Russia, Austria and Sweden against France.

1805   October 21. Admiral Nelson won the Battle of Trafalgar
which gave control of the seas back to Britain.

1806   March 28. Prussia in conformity with the Treaty of
February 15 with France, closed her ports to British
trade.

November 21. Napoleon issued the Berlin Decree pro-
claiming the whole of the British Isles in a state of
blockade; prohibited commerce with Britain; seized
British goods and declared British subjects prisoners of
war.

1807   January 27. Napoleon issued a decree at Warsaw, or-
dering seizure of all British goods in the Hanse Towns.

March 25. The slave trade was abolished by Parliament.

September 2. The English bombarded Copenhagen and
seized the Danish fleet.

1809   February. The <u>Quarterly</u> <u>Review</u> first appeared with
articles by Scott after he was estranged from the <u>Edin-</u>
<u>burgh</u> <u>Review</u>.

1811   February 5. The Regency Bill was passed because
                George III became insane. The regency was granted to
                the Prince of Wales with certain limitations.

1812   June 18. The United States declared war against Great
                Britain because of British search and seizure procedures
                of American ships. Napoleon had recalled his decrees
                on November 1, 1810 against American trade. The Liver-
                pool administration was to cancel restrictions on Ameri-
                can trade on June 23, but it was known in America in
                enough time.

1814   Sir Walter Scott published his first novel, Waverley.

                May 30. The first Treaty of Paris was signed. It out-
                lined the settlement of territorial questions in Europe in
                which France was concerned, aimed mainly at construc-
                tion of strong barrier to resist further encroachments by
                France on her neighbors. The French borders were to
                coincide with those of January 1, 1792.

                July 8. Alexander I, the Russian Tsar, and Frederick
                William, King of Prussia, visited England.

                September. The Congress of Vienna opened. It lasted
                until June 1815.

                December 24. The Treaty of Ghent was signed, ending
                the War of 1812 between American and Great Britain.

1815   George Stephenson invented the locomotive engine at
                Killingworth.

                January 3. A Secret Treaty was concluded between Aus-
                tria, France and Great Britain in defense of what they
                called "the principles of the peace of Paris." Each
                nation was to be prepared to put men in the field if
                Russia and Prussia pushed their territorial claims to
                the fullest extent.

                March 1. Napoleon returned from Elba. This was the
                beginning of the 100 days.

                June 18. The Battle of Waterloo was fought in which Na-
                poleon was defeated. He abdicated for the second time on
                June 22.

July 7. The allies occupied Paris. Napoleon finally surrendered to the British.

August 8. Napoleon set sail for St. Helena on board the
British ship, Northumberland. He protested against the
bad faith of Great Britain.

November 20. The Second Treaty of Paris was signed.
France was forced to surrender more territory. Britain
gained only a solemn denunciation of the slave trade.
Britain did gain some territory, including Heligoland and
the Ionian Islands. Austria, Britain, Prussia and Russia
signed a treaty, pledging themselves to act in case a
fresh revolution and usurpation in France should threaten
others.

1816   Coleridge published "Christabel" as well as "Kubla Khan"
              which had been written earlier.

              December 2. A meeting of reformers at Spa Fields was
              to be addressed by "Orator" Hunt, Major Cartwright and
              others. Watson led the mob who broke into a gunsmith's
              shop with some bloodshed. The Lord Mayor and a few
              assistants dispersed them. Fear spread in England.

1817   Blackwood's and London Magazine appeared. Thomas de
              Quincey wrote for both of them.

1819   August 16. The Peterloo Massacre occured at St. Peter's
              Fields outside of Manchester. Orator Hunt was to speak.
              Troops were brought up to disperse mob, fired and killed
              and wounded several people.

              December. The Six Acts were passed. Two were
              directed against the possession of arms and military
              training for unlawful purposes, two others were to curb
              freedom of the press, another to prevent seditious meet-
              ings, and one imposed a stamp-duty on small pamphlets.

1820   January 1. The Cato Street conspiracy was uncovered as
              a result of an informer. It was a plot by Arthur Thistle-
              wood to assassinate the ministers at a Cabinet dinner in
              Harrowby's house in Grosvenor Square. Thistlewood and
              several others escaped, but they were captured the next
              day.

              January 29. George III died. He was succeeded by
              George IV.

June 6. Queen Caroline returned to England after having lived a scandalous life abroad. She was welcomed by crowds. She was refused recognition by the King and was not crowned Queen. Caroline was eventually granted an annuity by the House of Commons.

October 20. The Congress of Troppau met to deal with Revolutions. Great Britain was opposed to joint interference.

1821   July 19. The coronation of George IV was held. Caroline was refused admittance.

August 7. Caroline died.

1822   August 12. Castlereagh died. Canning became foreign secretary in September.

October 20. The Congress of Verona was held. The Duke of Wellington offered mediation in regard to Spain.

1823   October. Czar Alexander of Russia and the Austrian Emperor Francis met in Bukowina to try to forestall the isolated intervention of Britain in the Greek Revolution.

December 2. United States President James Monroe pronounced the Monroe Doctrine in an address to Congress. It announced protection of the independence of the American continents.

1825   The Stockton and Darlington Railroad opened.

1826   Benjamin Disraeli published <u>Vivian Grey</u>.

December. The English sent troops to help the Portugese government against the insurgents.

1827   July 6. The Treaty of London was signed by France. Russia and Britain to settle the Greek question. It provided for a combination of the British, French and Russian fleets if Turkey did not agree to the sovereignty of Greece.

October 20. The Allied fleet entered the Bay of Navarino and fired upon the Turco-Egyptian fleet. The Allied fleet won a victory.

1828   London University was opened.

January 25. The Duke of Wellington accepted office as Prime Minister.

April 13. The Test and Corporation Acts were repealed, granting Catholic Emancipation when Daniel O'Connell was elected from an Irish constituency.

1830   June 26. George IV died. He was succeeded by William IV.

December 20. The Protocol of London was signed, providing for the separation of Belgium from Holland.

1831   September 8. The coronation of William IV was held.

November. The British and French fleets blockaded the Scheldt River.

December 12. The final Parliamentary Reform Bill was introduced, slightly reducing property requirements for voting, eliminating certain rotten boroughs, reducing the representatives of others and creating new boroughs.

1832   May 18. The Duke of Wellington and about 100 peers absented themselves so that the House of Lords could pass the Reform Bill.

June 7. The Reform Bill received the Royal assent.

1833   Sartor Resartus by Thomas Carlyle appeared.

Charles Lyell's Principles of Geology appeared.

The University of Durham was opened.

The Bill abolishing slavery in the colonies, with a period of apprenticeship, was passed.

The Factory Act was passed. No child under nine could be employed in a factory. After two years, none under 13 could work more than 48 hours and no one under 18 could work more than 69 hours a week.

March 21. A Convention was signed between Great
Britain, France and Holland, ending the embargo and
providing for free navigation of the Maas and Scheldt
Rivers.

April 22. The Quadruple Alliance of Britain, France,
Maria Christina, Queen Regent of Spain, and Peter, Re-
gent of Portugal, was signed. They agreed to expel Dom
Miguel, the Pretender of Portugal, and Don Carlos, the
Spanish Pretender, from the Portugese dominions. Great
Britain was to supply the necessary naval support and
France, the troops.

1834   February. The Poor Law Commissioners issued the report of their investigations. They found the evils of the
system to be almost universal.

August 4. The New Poor Law Amendment Act received
the royal assent, requiring that those who needed relief
be placed in workhouses. Only under the most extreme
conditions would outdoor relief be provided.

October 16. Fire destroyed the Houses of Parliament.
The Commons were able to meet in the House of Lords
Chamber.

December. Robert Peel formed a new ministry. Peel
issued the Tamworth manifesto, indicating the new conservative policy which accepted the Reform Act as a
final settlement of the constitutional question.

1835   April 8. Peel resigned after the January elections had
produced a hostile majority of Whigs and Irish. Melbourne formed his second ministry.

September 9. The Municipal Corporations Bill became
law, imposing a uniform constitutional form of government on all boroughs with the exception of the city of
London and a few of minor importance.

1836   Charles Dickens published Sketches by Boz.

A new Marriage Act was passed, maintaining the conditions of notice and publicity, but permitting civil as well
as religious wedding ceremonies.

August 17. The Registration Act was passed, constituting the clergymen of England as registrars for marriages they performed. It also permitted Dissenters to marry in their own Chapels.

1837   Charles Dickens began publication of Oliver Twist.

Thomas Carlyle's History of the French Revolution was published.

Chartism was initiated with its six-point program for Parliamentary reform.

June 1. The University of Durham was incorporated by Royal Charter.

June 20. King William IV died. Victoria succeeded to the throne.

THE VICTORIAN WORLD

1839   February. John G. Lambton, first Earl of Durham, with the aid of his secretary, Charles Buller, published his report on Canada.

May 7. Lord Melbourne in the Lords and John Russell in Commons announced the resignation of the ministry.

May 8. Robert Peel submitted his list of appointments to the government to Queen Victoria, indicating that there would have to be changes in the ladies of the royal household. Victoria refused and precipitated the bedchamber crisis. Peel would not take office, and Melbourne returned to office.

June. The Committee of the Council for education was constituted. The grant for education was increased from Ŀ20,000 to Ŀ30,000. Inspectors were to be appointed to supervise the administration of the grant.

1840   January 10. Uniform penny postage was introduced.

February 10. Queen Victoria married Prince Albert of Saxe-Coburg-Gotha.

July 28. The Canada Bill, uniting the two provinces and granting the assembly complete authority over colonial finances, was passed.

1841   August 30. After the elections, the Melbourne ministry was forced to resign. Peel formed a new government.

November 9. The future King Edward was born with the given name of Albert.

1842   January. The first Afghan war broke out.

August 9. The Webster-Ashburton Treaty was signed in which Britain apologized for the destruction of the Caroline in American waters. This prepared the way for a promise to the United States to help in the suppression of the slave trade.

1843   John Ruskin's Modern Painters appeared.

Second Report of children's employment was issued, showing that children of 6, 5, and even 4, were employed as apprentices.

1844   Disraeli's Coningsby was published.

October. King Louis Philippe of France visited Queen Victoria and Prince Albert at Windsor.

1845   Disraeli wrote Sybil.

August. The potato disease began in Ireland, which led to the great famine.

November 22. Lord John Russell announced his complete conversion to free trade.

December 5. Robert Peel resigned when his Cabinet would not support him on free trade. Lord John Russell would not form a government and Peel resumed office.

December 11. The First Sikh war began in India.

1846   Robert Browning married Elizabeth Barrett.

May 26. The House of Lords passed the Corn Law Bill establishing free trade. Robert Peel saw that he was being deserted by his own party because of his free trade stand and resigned on June 30.

June 14. The Oregon Boundary was settled.

1847   Jane Eyre by Charlotte Bronte was published. Emily
            Bronte's Wuthering Heights also appeared.

            William Makepeace Thackeray began publication of
            Vanity Fair.

1848   The first two volumes of Thomas Babington Macaulay's
            History of England from the Accession of James II was
            published.

            April 18. Third and last Chartist petition was presented.
            There was no major disturbance, although 170,000 spec-
            ial constables had been sworn in. Parliament rejected
            the petition when it was discovered that many of the
            signatures were forged.

1849   Charles Kingsley published two novels: Alton Locke and
            Yeast.

            The Navigation laws were repealed.

            March 29. The Sikh Wars were ended with the annexa-
            tion of Punjab.

1850   Charles Dickens' David Copperfield appeared.

            Alfred Lord Tennyson became Poet Laureate on the
            death of Wordsworth.

            The Australian Constitutions Act was passed, granting
            these colonies constitutional liberties.

            July 2. Sir Robert Peel died as a result of a fall from
            his horse.

1851   Stones of Venice by John Ruskin appeared.

            February 4. The Ecclesiastical Titles Bill was passed
            in order to resist Catholic ecclesiastical titles. It re-
            mained a dead letter, although it was not repealed until
            1871.

            May 1 - October 15. The Great Exhibition was held in
            Hyde Park. The Crystal Palace, which was the center
            of the Exhibition, was designed by Sir Joseph Paxton.

June. The "Don Pacifico" debate was held over Greek actions when the British intervened. Palmerston's program was defended.

December 19. Palmerston resigned. He brought about the resignation of the ministry on February 21, 1852. Lord Derby accepted the responsibility and formed a new government.

1852   Thackeray published Henry Esmond.

July. The Militia Bill was passed. The force was to be recruited by the voluntary enlistment. The ballot was to be retained for emergencies.

1853   April 18. William Ewart Gladstone presented his first budget.

1854   Dickens' Hard Times appeared.

March 12. A Treaty of Alliance between England, France and the Porte of Turkey was signed.

September 14. British and French troops landed in the Crimea. Many losses and indignities were suffered, as well as the suffering from diseases.

November 4. Miss Florence Nightingale and the first batch of nurses arrived at Constantinople on the way to the Crimea.

1855   Anthony Trollope published the first of his novels, The Warden.

February 1. The Aberdeen Ministry resigned as the result of attacks because of the manner in which they had been handling the war.

September 11. The Allies entered Sebastopol.

1856   February 13. The Oudh was annexed in India.

February 25. The Paris Peace Conference opened to arrange for the terms ending the Crimean War. The Treaty was signed March 30.

April 15. England, France and Austria signed a Treaty, giving their joint and separate guarantee of the independence and integrity of the Ottoman Empire.

November 1. England became involved in a war with Persia.

1857 George Eliot published <u>Adam</u> <u>Bede</u>.

March 4. The Persian War ended with a Treaty signed at Paris.

May 10. The Indian Mutiny broke out.

1858 Jewish Emancipation was granted.

William Morris published the <u>Defense</u> <u>of</u> <u>Guenevere</u>, a manifesto of the pre-Raphaelite poetry movement.

February 19. Palmerston was defeated on the Conspiracy to Murder Bill, because of the accusation that he was bowing before Napoleon III's demand. The second Derby Ministry was formed on March 1.

March 21. The British finally captured Lucknow, leading to the end of the Indian Mutiny.

August 22. The Government of India Bill became law, transferring powers of the East India Company to the Crown. It was officially carried out on November 1.

1859 Charles Dickens published <u>A</u> <u>Tale</u> <u>of</u> <u>Two</u> <u>Cities</u>.

Charles Darwin's <u>Origin</u> <u>of</u> <u>the</u> <u>Species</u> appeared.

Tennyson's <u>Idylls of the King</u> was published.

June 10. The Second Derby Ministry resigned.

1860 George Eliot published <u>Mill</u> <u>on</u> <u>the</u> <u>Floss</u>.

October 1. A Commercial Treaty with France was negotiated and completed by Richard Cobden, thereby bearing his name.

October 24. The Treaty of Pekin was signed, ending three years of war and difficult diplomacy.

1861 Silas Marner by George Eliot was published.

    December 14. Prince Consort Albert died.

1862 January 29. The Trent affair was settled when the United States released the Confederate Commissioners, Mason and Slidell, after having taken them off the British ship out of Savannah on November 9, 1861.

1863 Albert, the future Edward VII, married Princess Alexandre of Denmark.

1864 Algernon Charles Swinburne published Atalanta in Calydon.

1865 October 18. Lord Palmerston died.

1866 William Morris published The Earthly Paradise.

    June 18. The Government was defeated in the debate on the Reform Bill.

    June 26. Lord Derby became Prime Minister for the third time.

1867 March 8. Disraeli introduced his reform bill. All securities which were placed in the bill were forced out one by one. An extensive bill was finally passed.

    March 29. The Confederation of Canada was created.

1868 January 2. Robert Baron Napier landed in Abyssinia.

    February 25. Lord Derby resigned and was succeeded as Prime Minister by Benjamin Disraeli.

    December 2. The Conservative Government resigned as a result of a liberal victory at the general election. Gladstone formed a Liberal Ministry.

1869 William Lecky published his History of European Morals.

    James Anthony Froude completed his History of England from the Fall of Wolsey to the Spanish Armada.

March 1. The Irish Church Disestablishment Bill was introduced as a means of satisfying Irish discontent. It was passed in July.

1870   February 15. An Irish Land Bill was introduced. It interfered with the landlord's right of disposing of his land on the basis of free contract, but did not give the tenant fixity of tenure or security against excessive rents, nor did it take into account the fact that rents might be too high because of the decline of agriculture.

April 4. Irish Peace Preservation Act was passed.

August 9. The Education Bill received the royal assent. It permitted Anglican and Dissenting groups to form schools where they were lacking within one year. Local boards could then either support the existing schools or start new ones.

1871   George Eliot began publication of Middlemarch.

An act was passed, relieving members of Oxford and Cambridge from religious tests.

May 8. Treaty of Washington was signed, agreeing to settle Anglo-American differences. Alabama claims were to be settled by arbitrators.

November 1. A Royal Warrant announced the abolition of purchase of offices in the army.

1872   July 18. The Ballot Bill was passed, establishing the secret ballot.
September 14. An International Commission made the Geneva award, which favored the American claims.

1873   The Supreme Court of Judicature Act was passed.

February 14. The Irish University Bill was introduced. The University of Dublin was to be detached from Trinity College and reestablished as a teaching and examining body. It was not truly acceptable to the Irish, and the Liberals were lukewarm.

March 12-16. The Ministry was defeated and resigned, but it resumed office when Disraeli would not form a government.

1874   The Fiji Islands were annexed.

               Thomas Hardy's Far from the Madding Crowd appeared.

               January 26. Parliament was dissolved. The liberals
               were defeated in the elections in mid-February. Glad-
               stone resigned on February 17, and Disraeli formed his
               second government on the eighteenth.

1875   November 25. Disraeli arranged for the purchase of the
               Suez Canal shares from the Khedive Ismail of Egypt.

1876   May 13. The Berlin Memorandum was issued, indicating
               the concern of the three empires over the problems of
               Turkey and Bosnia and Herzegovina. It indicated the
               possibility of intervention. Disraeli repudiated the use
               of force.

               August 12. Disraeli became the Earl of Beaconsfield.

               December 11 - January 20, 1877. The Constantinople Con-
               ference met. The Turks thought that they could rely on
               British support against Russia. The Turks had already
               put down the Bulgarian uprising with much barbarity.
               The Conference failed.

1877   January 1. Victoria was proclaimed Empress of India.

               March 12. The Transvaal was annexed.

               October 31. The Irish National Land League was founded.

1878   Thomas Hardy published The Return of the Native.

               January 24. The British fleet entered the Dardanelles in
               order to try to bring an end to fighting in the Russo-Tur-
               kish War which had begun April 24.

               June 13 - July 13. The Congress of Berlin was held with
               Disraeli in attendance. Russia had to give up much of
               the territory which she had wrung from Turkey as a re-
               sult of the latter's defeat.

               July 4. Britain announced her agreement on June 4 to de-
               fend the Asiatic dominions of the Ottoman Empire "by
               force of arms." The Sultan agreed to introduce the
               necessary reforms.

1879   January 12. The Zulu War began. The Zulus were finally
defeated on July 3.

November 24. Gladstone in Midlothian announced some
of the themes upon which he planned to dwell in coming
electoral campaign against the Conservatives.

1880   April 18. Disraeli's government resigned after being defeated in elections. Shortly thereafter, Gladstone formed his third ministry.

December 16. The Transvaal rebellion began.

1882   April 19. Benjamin Disraeli, Earl of Beaconsfield, died.

May 2. William Forster resigned as Irish Secretary,
rather than to support a policy of releasing Charles
Stewart Parnell in return for his cooperation to bring
peace to Ireland. This was part of the "Treaty of Kil-
mainham."

May 6. Fenian assassins murdered Forster's successor, Lord Frederick Cavendish, and the permanent
under-secretary, Mr. Burke, in broad daylight in Phoe-
nix Park. The Government returned for a time to coercion. In the long run, it was going to try to create
peaceful conditions.

July. The Arrears Bill passed, which applied to tenan-
cies under Ł30. Obligations were to be cancelled if the
tenant had paid the rent for November 1880 - November
1881, and if they could prove to the land court that they
were unable to pay.

October. Irish National League was formed.

October 26. The Convention of London was ratified by
which the British gave in to some of the Boer demands in
order to end the Transvaal rebellion.

1883   Sir Henry James, the Attorney-general, introduced the
Corrupt Practices Bill, which was passed. It limited
the amount to be spent by a candidate or his agent in an
election.

1884   January 18. General Charles George Gordon was sent
                out to the Sudan. He was isolated at Khartoum on May
                26.

                July 15. Parliament resolved to send an expedition to re-
                lieve Khartoum.

                December. The Parliamentary Reform Bill was passed,
                greatly extending the vote.

1885   January 26. Khartoum fell to the Mahdi. Sir Charles Wil-
                son arrived with the relieving force on the twenty-eighth.

                March 20. The Russians attacked the Afghans at Penj-
                deh. A crisis developed which might have led to war be-
                tween Britain and Russia.

                April. The Sudan was evacuated.

                June 12. The Gladstone Government resigned when it
                was defeated on the budget resolutions.

                July 6. Lord Salisbury's new Conservative Ministry met
                with Parliament.

                December 17. Gladstone's plan to deal with the home
                rule issue for Ireland was revealed in the Press. He
                planned to achieve this without harming the unity of the
                empire. The Liberal Party began to have difficulties
                over this issue.

1886   February 1. Gladstone formed his fourth ministry after
                Salisbury's government had been forced to resign on
                January 28.

                March 26. Joseph Chamberlain and Sir George Trevelyan
                resigned from the Ministry because they refused to sup-
                port Home Rule.

                April 8. Gladstone introduced the Home Rule Bill.

                June 8. The Government was defeated on the second
                reading of the Home Rule Bill. Gladstone resigned on
                July 20.

July 26. Lord Salisbury agreed to form a government.

October 21. The Irish National League announced its "Plan of Campaign" for tenants to offer fair rents which if refused were to be given to a representative of the National League to be used for the campaign.

December 23. Lord Randolph Churchill resigned the post of Chancellor of the Exchequer and thus leadership of the House of Commons because of his opposition to armament expenditures.

1887   April-May. First Colonial Conference was held.

April 18. The Times published a letter dated May 15, 1882, which supposedly implicated Parnell in the murder of Lord Frederick Cavendish and Mr. Burke. A Commission was appointed which met from September 17, 1888 to November 22, 1889, and proved that the letters were forgeries and that Parnell was innocent.

June 21. Queen Victoria's Golden Jubilee was celebrated.

July 19. The Crimes Bill became law. Coercion was to be used because of increasing lawlessness in Ireland. The National League was declared a dangerous association on August 19.

1888   August 19. The County Councils Act was passed, establishing county councils throughout England and Wales. London was made a separate administrative county.

1889   October 29. A Charter was granted to the British South Africa Company.

1890   July 1. Lord Salisbury signed agreement with Germany settling the issues in Africa.

August 5. An agreement with France in regard to Africa was concluded.

November 17. Captain O'Shea obtained a decree nisi in a divorce court against his wife, naming Charles Stewart Parnell as correspondent. The Irish Party split over the issue because Gladstone and the Liberals could not support them with Parnell as their leader.

1891   Hardy's Tess of the d'Urbervilles was published.

                The Factory Act was passed, limiting the hours of labor
                for women to 12 hours per day with 1-1/2 hours for
                meals, as well as sanitary regulations. They raised the
                minimum working age for children to 11.

1892   August 15. Following the elections, Lord Salisbury re-
                signed after his government was defeated in a division
                on August 11.

                August 18. Gladstone formed his fourth ministry.

1893   February 13. The Second Home Rule Bill was introduced.
                It was passed in Commons, but rejected by the Lords on
                September 8.

1894   March 3. Gladstone resigned as Prime Minister at the
                age of 84. He was embittered over the opposition of the
                Lords to Irish Home Rule and other issues. Lord Rose-
                bery became Prime Minister.

1895   June 24. The Rosebery Government resigned when it
                was defeated on the issue of army estimates. Lord Sal-
                isbury formed a Conservative Ministry.

                July. General elections were held in which the Liberals
                were defeated.

                December 29 - January 2, 1896. Dr. L. S. Jameson,
                Administrator of Rhodesia, led a raid into the Transvaal.
                Jameson's men surrendered at Krugersdorf on January 2.

1896   January 3. The German Emperor, William II, sent
                President Kruger of the Transvaal a telegram congratu-
                lating him on repelling the invaders without calling for
                outside aid.

                January 6. Cecil Rhodes resigned the office of Premier
                of the Cape Colony. He resigned as a managing director
                of the Chartered Company on June 26. He had encouraged
                annexation of the Transvaal.

1897   June 22. Queen Victoria's 60th anniversary on the throne
                was celebrated.

1898   May 19. William Ewart Gladstone died.

                November 4. Major Marchand and his French troops
                withdrew from Fashoda after the British and the French
                came to an agreement in which the French gave way.

1899   Board of Education was set up under a Minister.

                January 19. The Cairo agreement was signed, placing
                the "Egyptian" Sudan under the condominium of England
                and Egypt.

                June. The Venezuela Boundary Commission met. It
                granted its award in October, vindicating the British
                claims in regard to British Guiana.

                October 11. The Boer War began. Peace was concluded
                at Vereeriging on June 1, 1902.

1900   February 27. The Labour Party was formed at a Con-
                ference under the leadership of Ramsay MacDonald.

                August. After a strike against the Taff Vale Railway,
                the company sued the union, the Amalgamated Society,
                which had to pay Ł23,000 in damages and an equal amount
                in costs. The Supreme Court of appelate jurisdiction in
                the Lords upheld the decision.

                Fall. General elections were held in which the Conserva-
                tives won a majority.

                           THE TWENTIETH CENTURY

1901   January 1. The Australian Commonwealth Act came into
                force. It was modeled on the Dominion of Canada Act of
                1867.

                January 22. Queen Victoria died. She was succeeded by
                Albert, who chose the name Edward VII.

1902   An Education Act was passed, setting up an education au-
                thority in every locality which was charged with super-
                vision of elementary, technical and secondary education.

January 30. The Anglo-Japanese Treaty was signed.
England was no longer isolated, and Japan was now an
equal with the greatest of the world empires.

July 11. Lord Salisbury resigned as Prime Minister.
Arthur Balfour succeeded him at the head of the Conservative Ministry.

August 9. The coronation of the King and Queen took
place. It has been postponed from June 26 when King
Edward had been operated on a few days before.

1903   May 15. Joseph Chamberlain delivered a speech at Birm-
ingham in which he called for imperial preference in
tariff policy.

September 9. In a letter to Balfour, Chamberlain sug-
gested his resignation so that he could devote full time to
explaining his concept of Imperial Union. Shortly thereafter, Chamberlain founded the Tariff Reform League.
He began the process of splitting the Conservatives as he
had previously split the Liberals.

1904   Arnold Forster proposed the Army Reorganization
Scheme.

The Licensing Act provided for financial compensation
when pub licenses were taken away, in order to reduce
the number of pubs.

April 8. An Anglo-French Entente was arranged settling
all colonial differences.

October 21. The Dogger Bank Incident occurred in which
the Russian fleet under Admiral Rodjestvensky fired on
a British fishing fleet with fatal results. The dispute was
submitted to an international commission.

1905   The Unemployed Workmen Act was passed.

December 4. Arthur Balfour resigned office as Conservative Prime Minister.

December 5. Sir Henry Campbell-Bannerman formed a
Liberal Ministry. Elections were held in which the
Liberals won.

1906   The Trades Disputes Act was passed, extending immu-
nity from criminal prosecution to the Unions the rights
which had been granted by the Conspiracy and Protection
of Property Act. It permitted peaceful picketing, removed liability for interfering with another person's
business and exempted the Trade Unions from all actions
for tort.

January 16. Algeciras Conference was held. It was a diplomatic bluff for Germany because England stood by her
entente partner, France, in retaining Morocco.

July 11. Joseph Chamberlain suffered a paralytic stroke
which ended his active career. He died July 2, 1914.

1907   Education Act was passed, providing for medical inspec-
tion of all school children.

June 19. Lord Haldane's Territorial and Reserve Forces
Act was passed. It went into operation March 31, 1908.
The goal was to provide the necessary forces which could
be called into active duty in the event of a major war.

August 31. The Anglo-Russian Treaty was signed,
settling all outstanding questions between the two states
in Central Asia.

1909   April 29. The Chancellor of the Exchequer, David Lloyd
George, introduced a budget which placed the charge for
social welfare legislation on the shoulders of the rich.
The Lords rejected the budget, opening up a struggle between the two Houses.

June. The Constitution for South Africa was ratified by
all constituent colonies.

December 2. Herbert Asquith proposed a resolution that
the refusal of the Lords to pass the budget was a breach
of the Constitution and usurpation of the rights of the
House of Commons. It was carried. Parliament was prorogued and then dissolved on January 10, 1910.

1910   January 15. In the elections, the Liberals won 274 seats to
the Conservatives' 273. Labour won 41 seats, and the
Irish Nationalists, 82. The latter two groups held the
balance.

March 29. Prime Minister Asquith introduced the Parliament Bill in three resolutions: 1. Money Bills were defined, and the Lords were to be prevented from rejecting or amending them; 2. Any Bill passed by Commons in three successive sessions and subsequently rejected by the Lords, provided that two years had elapsed since the introduction, should become law when royal assent was granted; and 3. The duration of Parliament was limited to five years.

April 29. The Budget of 1909 became law.

May 6. King Edward VII died. He was succeeded by his son, George V.

November 1. King George granted an interview to Mr. Asquith and Lord Crewe in which the King indicated that if the country were clearly in favor of the Parliament Bill, he would in the last resort create new Peers.

December. The second general election of 1910 was held. The Liberals and Unionists were tied with 272 seats each; Labour had 41, and the Irish Nationalists, 84. The latter were masters of the situation.

1911   July 1. The Germans informed the French that they had sent the gunboat, Panther, to Agadir to protect German lives after the French occupied Fez, the capital of Morocco, on May 21. The British took a firm attitude in support of France.

August 10. The House of Lords passed the Third Reading of the Parliament Bill, reducing their powers. Many Peers absented themselves in the face of the threat of the creation of additional peers.

The Commons passed a Bill providing for salaries for its members of Ł400 per year.

1912   Prime Minister, Asquith, submitted the Third Irish Home Rule Bill to the Commons. It received the Royal assent on September 18, 1914, but its implementation was delayed until after the war.

1913   February 1. The London Conference on the Balkans broke up with the outbreak of new fighting.

May 20. After the second armistice in the Balkans was concluded, negotiations reopened in London. Peace was signed before the end of May.

1914

May 19. The Bill to disestablish the Anglican Church in Wales went into effect after the third passage by the House of Commons under the Provisions of the Parliament Act of 1911.

June 28. The Archduke Franz Ferdinand, heir to the Austrian throne, and his wife were assassinated at Sarajevo by Bosnians.

July 31. The Stock Exchange closed until January 4, 1915 because of impending war.

August 2. The Cabinet met. The Unionist leaders indicated to Asquith the danger if Britain did not stand by Russia and France after Germany had declared war on both nations. Earl Grey asked Germany and France for a guarantee of Belgian neutrality, which Germany refused. The German invasion of Belgium made the war inevitable and helped Britain to enter the war as a united nation.

August 4. Britain declared war on Germany.

August. Defense of the Realm Act was passed, which gave the government the right to censor any paper, as well as cables and foreign correspondence.

August 19. Lord Kitchener sent the Fifth Division to France. He promised to send the Sixth as well on September 1. Eventually the entire regular army was sent to France as the British Expeditionary Force.

1915

January 13. The War Council resolved that the Admiralty should plan a campaign to take the Gallipoli Peninsula.

March 18. The British Fleet, along with French ships, entered the Straits. They were not sufficiently armed to complete the mission.

April. London was bombarded from the air.

April 25. British and Australian forces attacked Gallipoli, but the mission was a failure.

May 26. Asquith announced formation of a Coalition Government. Lloyd George was Minister of Munitions.

September 5-14. The Battle of the Marne was fought. Trench warfare began.

1916 January. The first Military Service Act was passed, imposing compulsory service on unmarried men between the ages of 18 and 41.

April 24. Irish uprising on Easter Sunday.

May 31. The Battle of Jutland was fought. The inconclusive result was disappointing to the British. The German fleet was not destroyed and the British suffered greater losses.

December 1. David Lloyd George proposed a War Council of three with himself in the chair. He obtained the support of Bonar Law, leader of the Conservatives. Asquith gave in on December 4. The ultimate result was that Lloyd George formed a new government.

1917 January. The Germans renewed unrestricted submarine warfare. President Wilson broke off relations with Germany, and the United States declared war against her in April.

April 30. Lloyd George took charge of the Admiralty and developed the convoy system.

November 6-7. Bolshevik Revolution occurred in Russia. The Russians eventually withdrew from the war.

November 18. The Balfour Declaration promised that Palestine should become a national home for the Jews.

1918 June. The Representation of the People Act was passed requiring a six months' residence for men over 21 in order to vote. Women over 30 were granted the vote.

July. Allied forces began to intervene in Russia.

September 29. General Ludendorff told the German Government that they must seek an armistice immediately.

November 11. The German delegation signed the armistice in France.

December 14. A general election was held. Lloyd George tried to maintain the coalition. It was accepted by the Conservative Unionists but not by the Labour Party. "Coupon" candidates had endorsement of Lloyd George and Bonar Law. The Coalition won a sweeping triumph, with 339 Unionists and 136 Liberals elected.

1919 January. Irish National volunteers were reorganized as the Irish Republican Army to war against Britain.

June 28. The Peace Treaty with Germany was signed at Versailles.

June. The Sankey Commission came up with four reports in regard to the mines, ranging from the complete nationalization by the workers' representatives to restoration of undiluted private ownership on the part of the owners. On August 18, Lloyd George used the excuse of disagreement to reject nationalization. He offered reorganization.

1920 Unemployment Insurance was extended to all workers earning less than Ł5 per week.

October. The miners went out on strike while the government was in control of the mines.

December 23. The Government of Ireland Act provided for two Home Rule Parliaments: one for most of Ireland at Dublin, and the other, for the six counties of Ulster at Belfast.

1921 April 1. Lockout by mine owners began. Miners called on their allies, the railway and transport unions for a sympathy strike. The strike, planned for April 15, was called off a few hours before it was to begin. The miners held on alone until July 1, when they returned on worse terms. Their defeat set the general pattern for every industry in 1921.

July 8. Eamon De Valera, President of the Irish Republic, signed a truce. The fighting ended three days later.

December 6. A Treaty was signed with the Irish implicitly recognizing the right of the Dail or its representatives to speak for the republic of United Ireland. The Parliament approved on December 16, and the Dail on January 7, 1922. The Irish disappeared from Westminster.

1922

October 19. A majority of the Conservatives decided to fight the election as an independent Party. Lloyd George resigned as Prime Minister.

October 23. Bonar Law was elected leader of the Conservative Party and then accepted the office of Prime Minister.

November 17. The Conservatives won the General election.

December. The British Broadcasting Company was formed. It was financed by a group of manufacturers who were given an exclusive license to broadcast.

1923

May 20. Bonar Law resigned as Prime Minister after he learned that he had incurable cancer of the throat. He died October 30.

May 22. Stanley Baldwin became Prime Minister. He was elected leader of the Conservatives on May 28.

July. Chamberlain's Housing Act was passed, granting a subsidy of Ł6 per year for 20 years to both public and private builders.

1924

January 23. Ramsay MacDonald became Prime Minister the day after the Conservatives were defeated in Parliament. It was the first Labour Government.

June. Stanley Baldwin renounced Protection, thus enabling the Liberals to vote for the Conservatives and defeat the Labor Government. Winston Churchill became Chancellor of the Exchequer. Austen Chamberlain was Foreign Secretary.

October 25. The Zinoviev letter was published. It was
allegedly written by the President of the Communist International to the British Party with instructions for seditious activities. It did hurt Labor chances in the election.

1925   June 30. The mine owners gave a month's notice that
they would end the existing agreement with the miners
and offered them sharply reduced wages. The miners refused and the Government then stepped in, agreeing to
grant a subsidy for 9 months while a Royal Commission,
under Sir Herbert Samuel, investigated the situation.

1926   March 11. The Samuel Commission issued its report on
the coal industry, proposing nationalization of royalties,
amalgamation of smaller pits, and better working conditions in the future. The only present recommendation
was an immediate reduction of wages. The owners accepted only the last part of the report.

May 1. The miners were locked out. A special Trade
Union conference approved plans for a national strike on
May 3.'

May 3. The General Strike broke out. The unions, as
well as the government, had prepared well. Volunteers
provided transportation for goods. The unions worked to
maintain peace and order.

May 12. The General Council called off the national
strike unconditionally. The miners were finally driven
back to work by starvation after holding out for six
months.

1927   May. The Government introduced a bill to amend the
Trades Dispute Act, making sympathetic strikes or
strikes designed or calculated to coerce the government
illegal. It also prohibited civil servants from joining a
union and required that members of unions who wanted
to pay a political levy had to contract in rather than having those who did not want to contract out. The act was
repealed shortly after the Labor victory in 1945.

1928   April. An act was passed, lowering the voting age for
women from 30 to 21.

August 27. Britain, along with other nations, signed the Kellogg Peace Pact.

1929

May. Elections were held in which the three parties fought each other for the first and last time. Labor won 288 seats, the Conservatives, 260, and Liberals only 59 seats.

June 5. Ramsay MacDonald became Prime Minister for the second time.

July. Lord Beaverbrook launched his crusade for Empire Free Trade.

October 3. MacDonald's government resumed diplomatic relations with the Soviet Union.

1930

MacDonald presided over the London Naval Conference which established the ratio for cruiser, submarines and destroyers at 5:5:3 for Great Britain, the United States and Japan.

The Coal Mines Act was passed, establishing a 7-1/4 hour day. The owners were empowered to fix minimum prices and quotas of production.

June 24. The Simon Commission issued its report on India, recommending responsible government in the provinces.

October 30. The Colonial Secretary, Lord Passfield, announced in a White Paper that Jewish immigration to Palestine must virtually cease because of Arab resistance.

1931

July 31. The May Committee report was issued by the Committee under Sir George May. It recommended that only part of the government's budget deficit be covered by additional taxation, and that the remainder be removed through economies.

August 11. Bankers met with Prime Minister MacDonald and indicated that they would only grant the government loans if economies were made.

August 25. The National Government was formed with Ramsay MacDonald as Prime Minister. The majority of the Labor Party refused to go along and eventually expelled MacDonald from the Party.

September 18. Japan attacked Manchuria.

September 21. The Act, suspending the gold standard, was rushed through Parliament.

October 27. General elections were held. The Conservatives with their allies, the National Labor Party (Mac-Donaldites) and the National Liberals (Simonites) won 521 seats.

December 11. The Statute of Westminster was passed, granting legislative freedom to Canada, Australia, New Zealand, Ireland and Newfoundland.

1932   Oswald Mosley founded the British Union of Fascists.

December. The British paid an installment on war debts to the United States as a gesture of solvency when others were not paying. They made a token payment in June of 1933 and then gave up.

1933   February. Famous resolution was passed at Oxford Union that "this House will not fight for King and Country." It was a gesture of loyalty to world peace, rather than disloyalty to Great Britain.

June 12. The World Economic Conference opened in the Geological Museum at South Kensington. It was attended by representatives of almost every government.

July 5. President Roosevelt killed the World Economic Conference by refusing to stabilize the dollar.

November 1. The Labor Party won control of 200 boroughs at municipal elections.

1935   Watson Watt invented radar.

January 1. New National rates for unemployment payments went into effect. It was less than those fixed by local public assistance committees in many cases.

March 4. A White Paper, Statement Relating to Defense, was issued. It announced that the British government ceased to rely on collective security and was now going to rely on armed force. Hitler used this pronouncement as an excuse for restoring conscription in Germany on March 16.

April 11. MacDonald met with Benito Mussolini, Italian
Duce, and Pierre Laval, French Prime Minister, and
set up the Stresa front against breaches of international
order.

June 18. The National Government made a private deal with
Germany, limiting the German navy to 35% of the British
and submarines to 45% or 100% in case of danger from
Russia.

August 2. The Government of India Act became law. It
provided for responsible government in the provinces and
the central power under the control of the British viceroy.

November 14. General elections were held. The Conservatives held almost exactly their vote of 1931, with
Labor increasing its seats.

December 7. Sir Samuel Hoare and Pierre Laval en-
dorsed the Hoare-Laval Plan, under which Italy was to
receive the fertile plains of Ethopia, and Emperor Haile
Selassie would keep his kingdom in the mountains. A
public outcry forced them to back down and eventually resign.

1936   January 20. George V died. He was succeeded by Edward VIII.

July 16. The Spanish Civil War began. The British and
French governments proposed a general agreement not to
aid either side in Spain. The other powers agreed, but
the Germans and Italians aided the insurgents.

December 10. Edward VIII abdicated when he could not
obtain agreement to marry Mrs. Wallis Warfield Simpson, a double divorcee. He was succeeded by his brother, George VI.

1937   A new Irish constitution was devised by Eamon De Valera
which made Eire, Southern Ireland, independent for all
practical purposes.

January 2. The Mediterranean Agreement was signed between Great Britain and Italy, agreeing to the status quo
in the area.

February 20. Anthony Eden resigned as Foreign Minister.

May. Stanley Baldwin resigned as Prime Minister. He was succeeded by Neville Chamberlain.

July 7. A Royal Commission, under Lord Peel, recommended partition of Palestine into an Arab State, a Jewish State and a British mandate for Jerusalem and Bethlehem with a corridor to the sea.

1938   September 15. Prime Minister Chamberlain took his first plane trip to Munich, met Hitler at Berchtesgaden, offered the separation of the Sudeten Germans from the rest of Czechoslovakia.

September 18. French Premier Edouard Daladier and Foreign Minister Bonnet to London. Daladier forced Chamberlain to agree to guarantee a weakened Czechoslovakia. President Benes agreed on September 21, because of the ultimatum that otherwise Great Britain and France would not support him.

September 22. Chamberlain flew to Germany, met with Hitler at Godesburg, where the latter wanted immediate occupation. Finally, Hitler agreed not to act before October 1. Chamberlain returned home.

September 29. Chamberlain flew to Munich again to a four-power conference arranged by Mussolini. The agreement reached was that the occupation of the Sudeten territories would be spread over ten days instead of at once. Czechoslovakia was to be guaranteed by the four Powers after the issue of the Polish and Hungarian minorities was settled. The agreement was reached shortly after midnight on September 30.

September 30. Chamberlain arrived back in England, claiming "I believe it is peace in our time."

1939   February 27. The British Government recognized Franco as the rightful ruler of Spain.

March 15. Hitler helped to make Czechoslovakia fall to pieces.

March 19. Chamberlain drafted a declaration of joint
resistance which French, Polish and Soviet governments
were invited to sign. The Russians agreed only if the
French and Poles signed first. The Poles refused because they would not take sides between Russia and Germany.

March 31. Chamberlain wrote an assurance to the Poles
that his government would aid them if their independence
were threatened by Germany. The actual alliance was
not signed until August 25.

August 12-21. Final stages of negotiations with Russia
in the form of military talks were held.

August 23. Nazi-Soviet Non-Aggression Pact was signed.

August 24. Parliament passed the Emergency Powers
Act.

August 25. The Anglo-Polish Treaty of mutual assistance was signed.

August 31. Hitler gave the order to attack Poland. German troops crossed the Polish frontier on September 1.

September 3. A British ultimatum was delivered to Germany to withdraw from Poland. When no reply was received by 11 A.M., Britain declared war. France declared war at 5 P.M. The British colonies and India
were automatically at war. The Dominions had freedom
of choice.

September 6. General Smuts became Prime Minister of
South Africa after Herzog resigned. South Africa then
declared war.

December. British ships forced the Graf Spee to take
refuge in Montevideo, where it was scuttled on Hitler's
orders.

1940   January 9. Rationing of bacon, ham, butter and sugar
began.

January 22. The celebration of the 100th anniversary of
the landing of the first white settlers in New Zealand began at Wellington.

February 12. 30,000 troops from Australia and New
Zealand landed at Suez, bringing to 570,000 the number
of British and French troops in the Near East.

February 15. Great Britain offered to use its warships to
convoy neutral vessels in order to protect them from German submarines.

February 23. A British-French squadron of warships began a blockade of the north coast of Norway, Sweden and
Russia.

February 28. The government issued orders, prohibiting Jews from buying land in one part of Palestine and
restricting their purchases in another.

March 28. The Supreme War Council of the Allies met
in London and resolved that neither France nor Great
Britain would make a separate peace.

May 10. British forces landed in Iceland.

The Germans invaded Belgium, Holland and Luxembourg.

Chamberlain resigned as Prime Minister and Winston
Churchill was commissioned as his successor.

May 22. Parliament authorized the Government to take
control of all industry, property and labor needed to
win the war.

May 31. London announced that three-fourths of the
British Expeditionary Force in Flanders had been safely
evacuated from Dunkirk.

June 10. Premier Mussolini of Italy declared war against
England and France.

June 18. German planes made their first concerted attack
on Britain.

June 23. The French National Committee, led by General
Charles de Gaulle, was formed in London. It was recognized as the leader of all "free" Frenchmen and an ally
by the British government on June 28.

July 10. The Government recognized Haile Selassie as Emperor of Ethiopia.

July 30. Britain extended its naval blockade to include all of continental Europe.

August 16. Metropolitan London was heavily bombed.

August 26. The British made the first bombing attack on Berlin.

September. President Roosevelt announced the bases for destroyer deal with Britain.

September 11. The British damaged the Reichstag Building in a raid on Berlin.

October 8. Prime Minister Churchill announced that the Burma Road, which had been closed July 7, would be re-opened October 17.

December 10. The Government announced that it would refuse permission for shipment of food to the Continent through the blockade.

December 23. Viscount Halifax was appointed British ambassador to the United States, succeeding the late Lord Lothian. Anthony Eden was named Foreign Secretary.

1941   January 22. Tobruk fell to the British after a 36-hour attack.

February 10. Britain broke off diplomatic relations with Rumania.

March 12. Prime Minister Churchill thanked the United States for enacting the Lend-Lease Bill, terming it the "new Magna Carta."

April 7. London severed diplomatic relations with Budapest, Hungary.

April 19. The British landed strong forces in Iraq to guard the Mosul oilfields.

April 30. The British succeeded in evacuating 48,000 of the 60,000 troops which had originally landed in Greece.

May 11. The Nazis bombed London, destroying the House of Commons Chamber and damaging Westminster Abbey.

May 24. The British sank the German Battleship, Bismarck.

May 31. An armistice was signed in Baghdad between Britain and Iraq ending the month-long war.

The Board of Trade announced that it had abandoned Crete to the Axis.

June 8. An allied force of British and Free French troops invaded Syria from three points.

June 22. Germany invaded the U.S.S.R. on three fronts. Prime Minister Churchill promised economic and technical aid for Russia.

July 11. An armistice to end the war in Syria was concluded between the British and the Free French forces on the one side and the Vichy command on the other.

July 13. Britain and Russia signed a mutual aid pact agreeing not to sign a peace pact without mutual consent. A Trade Pact was signed on August 17.

July 25. The United States and Britain froze all Japanese assets to stop further Nipponese aggression.

August 14. Prime Minister Churchill and President Roosevelt met on a British Battleship in the Atlantic. They agreed on the Atlantic Charter, an eight-point declaration of war and peace aims.

August 24. Prime Minister Churchill told Japan that Britain would side with the United States in event of trouble in the Far East.

November 18. British forces landed in Libya.

December 6. Britain declared war on Finland, Hungary and Rumania.

December 8. Prime Minister Churchill declared war on
Japan, as did the United States following the Japanese
attack on Pearl Harbor on December 7.

December 16. The British command in Hong Kong admitted evacuating the mainland section on the night of
December 11-12.

1942   January 2. Representatives of all 26 nations at war with
the Axis signed the "Declaration by the United Nations"
in Washington for a united war and peace.

February 15. Singapore surrendered to the Japanese.

February 23. The United States and Britain in a joint declaration signed by Lord Halifax and Sumner Welles,
American Under-Secretary of State, agreed to create a
liberal economic international system after the war.

March 29. Sir Stafford Cripps revealed the British plan
to offer India complete dominion status after the war in
return for Indian cooperation against the Axis.

April 12. Pandit Nehru said that India would develop its
own war effort instead of participating in Britain's.

May 26. Britain and Russia signed a 20-year mutual
assistance treaty banning a separate peace with Germany.

June 25. The United States established headquarters in
England for the European Theatre of Operations under
Major General Dwight D. Eisenhower.

October 9. The United States and Britain announced plans
to relinquish their territorial rights in China.

November 5. Lieutenant General B. L. Montgomery
announced a British victory in Egypt.

1943   January 14. President Roosevelt and Prime Minister
Churchill met in Casablanca to confer on war strategy.

January 23. Tripoli fell to the British 8th Army.

March 21. Prime Minister Churchill proposed postwar
councils for Europe and Asia.

April 7. Lord Keynes' proposal for postwar currency and banking was published in a British White Paper.

April 30. A new British-Canadian plan for convoy protection in the North Atlantic was announced, including an "air umbrella".

July 10. American, British and Canadian troops invaded Sicily.

August 17. All Sicily fell to the Allied armies.

August 17-24. Roosevelt and Churchill conferred in Quebec.

November 26. President Roosevelt, Prime Minister Churchill and Generalissimo Chiang Kai-shek completed a five-day conference in Cairo, concerning the war with Japan and peace plans.

December 1. President Roosevelt, Premier Stalin and Prime Minister Churchill completed a 4-day conference in Teheran, reaching agreement on plans to defeat Germany and establishing a post-war peace organization.

1944

January 22. British and American troops landed on the west coast of Italy.

March 12. All travel between Britain and Ireland was suspended to conceal invasion maneuvers.

March 23. British imposed a curfew on the Jewish sections of the chief Palestine cities after terrorists killed six policemen and wounded twelve others.

June 6. The allied invasion of Western Europe was launched.

June 15. England was attacked for the first time by pilotless robot bombs which were launched from the Pas-de-Calais area.

August 29. At the Dumbarton Oaks Conference, representatives of the United States, Britain and Russia reached a general agreement on the structure and aims of an international league to preserve peace.

September 16. Roosevelt and Churchill concluded the second parley, pledging a shift of war to the Pacific after the defeat of Germany.

October 9. The Big Four: United States, Britain, Russia and China announced that the Dumbarton Oaks Conferees would recommend creation of the United Nations.

October 25. The United States and Britain gave diplomatic recognition to Italy after Mussolini had been overthrown.

November 24. The United States, Britain and Russia agreed to coordinate their policies for postwar occupation and administration of Germany.

1945   February 4-11. The Yalta Conference was held in which President Roosevelt, Prime Minister Churchill and Premier Stalin agreed on crushing Nazism and German militarism; establishing popular governments in liberated countries; requiring Germany to pay reparations in kind for war damages; setting up occupation zones in Germany; calling a United Nations Conference at San Francisco, California on April 25 and broadening the base of the Polish and Yugoslav governments.

May 2. The Germans surrendered in Italy.

May 7. Germany surrendered unconditionally. It was formally ratified in Berlin, May 8.

July 26. The Labor Party won elections upon which they had insisted following the defeat of Germany. Clement R. Attlee became Prime Minister.

August 2. President Truman, who had succeeded President Roosevelt after his death in April, Prime Minister Attlee, and Premier Stalin reached an agreement at the Potsdam Conference on German industry and reparations, as well as annexation of East Prussia by Poland and the Soviet Union.

August 8. Representatives of the United States, Great Britain, France and Russia agreed on a new international code, defining war as a crime against the world.

August 14. The Japanese accepted the Allied unconditional surrender terms.

September 19. Lord Haw Haw, William Joyce, who had broadcast for the Nazis, was sentenced to be hung for treason. He was executed January 3.

November 7. The world air speed record of 606 miles per hour was claimed for a British jet plane.

December 6. An Anglo-American financial pact was signed, granting Britain $4.4 billion for an early resumption of world trade.

1946

April 30. An Anglo-American committee of inquiry into the problems of the Jews in Europe and Palestine, recommended that 100,000 Jews be permitted entry into Palestine as soon as possible.

May 16. British White Paper set forth a six-point plan as the basis for a constitution to be drafted by the Indians, rejecting the Moslem demand for a separate state of Pakistan.

June 5. Winston Churchill supported the Labor Government's foreign policy in the House of Commons debate, charging that the seeds of World War III were being sown in Russian-occupied Europe.

July 3. The British Food Minister, John Strachey, told the House of Commons that Britain had introduced bread rationing because of the fear that American labor problems might stop wheat exports.

August 12. The British government announced a halt on all illegal immigration of Jews to Palestine, saying that would-be immigrants would be interned in Cyprus.

October 4. The Labor Government announced the formation of a new ministry of defense, intended to coordinate all the armed forces.

November 6. The National Health Service Act and The Coal Industry Nationalization Act were passed.

1947   February 20. The British announced their intention to
            withdraw from India by June 1948. The Commons ap-
            proved on March 6.

            March 4. France and Britain signed a 50-year treaty of
            alliance in Dunkirk ceremony.

            August 6. The Transportation Industry was nationalized.

            August 15. Britain's long rule over India was formally
            ended with the establishment of India and Pakistan.
            Arthur Henderson was appointed Minister of State for
            Commonwealth relations.

            August 27. "Siege economy" measures were passed,
            placing food, motoring and foreign travel under severe
            rationing.

            August 31. The British termination of their mandate in
            Palestine, and its partition into Arab and Jewish states
            was recommended by the majority of the United Nations
            Special Committee on Palestine. The British began to
            evacuate their troops on November 16.

            November 1. The Labor Party was decisively defeated by
            the Conservatives in municipal elections in England and
            Wales. The Labor Government refused to call for gen-
            eral elections.

            November 20. Princess Elizabeth, heiress presumptive
            to the throne, and Prince Philip, Duke of Edinburgh, were
            married.

            December 11. Russia and Britain reached an agreement
            on a trade pact.

1948   January 1. Nationalization of the railways, canals and
            adjuncts took place under the 1947 Transport Act. The
            Transport Commission took charge, under Sir Cyril
            Hurcomb.

            February 4. The Government called for a voluntary
            freeze of wages to combat inflation.

            February 12. Chancellor of the Exchequer, Sir Stafford
            Cripps, announced the freezing of prices at the level at
            the end of 1947.

February 18. British physicians voted overwhelmingly to refuse to join the free medical service system set up by the National Health Service Act.

March 15. Britain and Trans-Jordan concluded a new military treaty.

March 17. The Government signed a 50-year treaty of mutual aid and economic and social cooperation in Brussels with Belgium, France, Luxembourg and the Netherlands.

April 1. The Electricity Authority, headed by Lord Citrine, assumed control of Britain's nationalized electricity industry. The Act had been passed August 13, 1947.

April 29. The Palestine Act was passed, terminating the British mandate.

May 15. The British mandate in Palestine expired one minute past midnight. The Arab states invaded the country. The last British troops were withdrawn on June 30.

June 2. American and British authorities in Germany instituted the airlift to supply Berlin.

July 5. The Labor Government's comprehensive national health and social security program went into operation.

August 14. The XIV Olympiad ended in London.

November 14. Princess Elizabeth gave birth to a son, who was christened Prince Charles on December 15.

1949   January 6. The Prime Ministers of Great Britain and Northern Ireland reaffirmed that the latter's constitutional status would not be changed without its consent.

January 29. The Foreign Office announced defacto recognition of the State of Israel.

May 1. The gas industry passed into public ownership.

May 12. The House of Commons ratified the North Atlantic Treaty.

The Berlin Blockade was lifted at 12:01 A.M. Berlin time.

September 18. The Chancellor of the Exchequer announced devaluation of the pound sterling from $4.03 to $2.80.

November 16. The House of Commons approved an amended bill for nationalizing the Steel Industry which postponed the date until January 1, 1951. The House of Lords gave final approval on November 24.

1950

February 23. The Labor Party won a narrow Parliamentary victory. Attlee announced the decision of the Labor Government to remain in office.

April 27. The Government gave de jure recognition to Israel and also recognized annexation by Jordan of that part of Palestine under Jordani control.

June 18. The Government announced cancellation of all petroleum shipments to Communist China.

1951

February 15. The major part of the iron and steel industry passed into government ownership under the aegis of the government-owned Iron and Steel Corporation headed by Steven J. L. Hardie. The Act had been passed November 24, 1949.

September 23. King George VI was reported in satisfactory condition following a major operation for a lung resection.

October 16. British troops occupied Port Said at the northern terminus of the Suez Canal after anti-British rioting broke out.

October 25. The Conservative Party defeated the Labor Party in Parliamentary elections. Winston Churchill, leader of the Conservatives, was designated Prime Minister by King George VI on October 26.

November 5. King George VI conferred the Order of Merit on former Prime Minister Clement Attlee.

December 31. The United Kingdom paid the first installment on a 1946 loan and World War II debt to the United
States.

1952
February 6. King George VI died unexpectedly. His
eldest daughter was proclaimed Queen Elizabeth II by
the Privy Council. George VI was buried February 15.

February 17. Prime Minister Churchill announced that
the United Kingdom would test an atomic weapon in Australia some time in 1952.

March 28. The House of Commons approved proposals
to charge for prescriptions, as well as some surgical
appliances and dental services, under the national health
program.

April 11. Queen Elizabeth II decreed that she, her
children and their children would retain the family name
of Windsor.

May 21. The House of Commons voted approval of the
return of the long-distance trucking industry to private
ownership.

September 14. Former Prime Minister Attlee pledged
that when the Labor Party returned to office, it would
re-nationalize all industries returned to private hands
by the Conservatives.

October 3. Britain's first atomic weapon was success-
fully exploded in the Monte Bello Islands, 50 miles north-
west of Australia.

October 20. Authorities declared a state of emergency
in Kenya in an effort to control the anti-white Mau Mau
Society.

November 15. The Colonial Office announced that the
colonies of Jamaica, Trinidad; the Leeward and the Wind-
ward Islands had agreed to form a Federation.

1953
February 23. Prime Minister Churchill announced a
general coronation year amnesty for deserters from the
British armed forces during World War II.

April 24. Prime Minister Churchill was made a Knight
of the Garter, the highest and oldest British order of
Knighthood, by Queen Elizabeth II.

May 6. Queen Elizabeth II gave her royal assent to the
bill denationalizing the motor transport industry.

May 14. Queen Elizabeth II gave her royal assent to the
bill denationalizing the iron and steel industry.

June 2. The coronation of Queen Elizabeth II was held
at Westminster Abbey, London,

October 6. The Colonial Office announced the despatch
of troops to British Guiana to forestall a suspected Communist coup. The Commons approved suspension of the
Constitution on October 22.

December 8. Prime Minister Churchill, President Eisenhower and French Premier Joseph Laniel, at the Bermuda
Conference, issued a communiqué reaffirming N.A.T.O.
as the foundation of their policy and stating that they approved a four-power conference with the U.S.S.R.

1954   February 18. The government announced that atomic
weapons were in production.

May 6. Roger Bannister of England became the first
person to run the mile in less than 4 minutes in a track
meet at Oxford, England. The time was 3 minutes, 59.4
seconds.

May 8. Government representatives attended the Geneva
Conference on Indochina.

July 30. Minister of Supply, Duncan Sandys, announced
that the American and British governments had formally
approved arrangements for closer collaboration on
guided missiles.

October 19. Egypt and the United Kingdom signed a formal agreement in Cairo designed to restore control of
the Suez Canal Zone to Egypt.

1955   February 17. The Government announced its ability and intention to produce a hydrogen bomb.

April 6. Queen Elizabeth II named Sir Anthony Eden to replace Sir Winston Churchill, who had resigned, as Prime Minister.

June 15. Britain and the United States signed agreements for cooperation in civil uses of atomic energy and in the use of atomic information for mutual defense purposes.

July 25. Chancellor of the Exchequer, R. A. Butler, announced new restrictions on credit designed to reduce domestic consumption and increase exports.

September 22. The first television program, financed by advertising, was telecast from London.

November 9. Prime Minister Eden offered his services and those of his government in settling the dispute between Israel and the Arab States.

December 3. Britain and Egypt signed an agreement in Cairo, granting to the Sudan the right of self-determination.

December 7. Clement R. Attlee resigned the leadership of the Labor Party and was made an earl by Queen Elizabeth II. Hugh Gaitskell was named to succeed Atlee on December 14.

1956   February 11. Former diplomats, Guy Burgess and Donald Maclean, who had disappeared in 1951, reappeared at a press conference in Moscow.

May 11. Colonial Secretary Lennox-Boyd announced that Britain was prepared to grant the Gold Coast independence if its newly-elected legislature so requested.

May 21. Foreign Secretary Selwyn Lloyd declared that Britain would retain Cyprus and other strategic points, by force, if necessary.

June 13. Britain's 74-year occupation of the Suez Canal ended.

July 20. The Government withdrew its offer to help Egypt
construct the proposed Aswan Dam.

July 26. The Egyptian Government seized the Suez Canal
and nationalized the Suez Canal Company. The British
Treasury blocked all Egyptian accounts in the United
Kingdom on July 28.

August 9. Britain initiated a major airlift of the troops
to the Middle East.

August 16. The London Conference on the status of the
Suez Canal opened. On August 23, 18 of the 22 nations
attending asked Egypt to negotiate with a five-power committee for international control of the Suez Canal. President Nasser agreed on August 28, but the negotiations
were announced a failure on September 9.

September 23. The British and French governments
called for a Security Council meeting to consider the
Suez Canal situation.

October 12. The British, Egyptian and French foreign
ministers agreed in New York City upon six general
principles to govern the operation of the Suez Canal but
remained deadlocked on the question of control.

October 17. Queen Elizabeth II opened the world's first
full-scale nuclear power station at Calder Hall, England.

October 31. The British bombed airfields in Egypt, beginning the invasion of Egypt with the French.

November 7. Britain and France began a cease-fire in
Egypt at 2 A.M. Egyptian time.

November 13. Colonial Secretary Lennox-Boyd announced
termination of British military operations against the Mau
Mau in Kenya.

December 3. The British and French governments
pledged complete withdrawal of their troops from Egypt
without delay. The evacuation was completed December
22.

December 19. The Government issued a White Paper, proposing limited self-government for Cyprus.

1957   January 9. Prime Minister Sir Anthony Eden resigned on grounds of ill-health and also because of the crisis connected with the invasion of the Suez Canal Zone. Queen Elizabeth II named Harold Macmillan, Prime Minister.

February 7. Royal assent was given to the act, granting independence to Ghana (the former Gold Coast) within the Commonwealth.

February 22. Queen Elizabeth II bestowed the title of Prince of the United Kingdom upon her husband, Philip.

March 21. A law, introducing a number of basic changes in the British law of murder and restricting cases in which the death penalty could be imposed, took effect immediately after receiving the royal assent.

March 24. President Eisenhower and Prime Minister Macmillan issued a joint communiqué at the end of their Bermuda Conference, stating that the United States agreed to supply guided missiles to Britain.

April 4. The Government announced in a White Paper a sharp change in its defense policy with primary reliance on nuclear weapons in the future.

May 15. The government announced the first in a series of nuclear tests.

July 6. The last British troops left Jordan.

November 5. Queen Elizabeth II announced in her speech from the throne the intention of her government to introduce legislation for the creation of life peerages, with the right to sit and vote in the House of Lords, for both men and women. The Act received royal assent on April 30, 1958.

December 7. Troops arrived in British Honduras following the disclosure of an alleged plot for union with Guatemala.

1958   February 22. The United States and Britain signed in
                Washington, D. C. a 50-year agreement for supplying
                American intermediate-range ballistic missiles to
                Britain.

                February 26. British European Airways and the Soviet
                Aeroflot signed an agreement in Moscow for direct Lon-
                don to Moscow air service.

                April 13. Colonial Secretary Lennox-Boyd announced in
                Nassau labor and electoral reforms to alleviate unrest in
                the Bahamas.

                April 22. Princess Margaret formally inaugurated the
                first parliament of the West Indies in Port-of-Spain,
                Trinidad.

                June 19. The government offered "Partnership" rule to
                Greece, Turkey and the Cypriots as a solution to the
                Cyprus situation.

                July 17. Prime Minister Macmillan informed the House
                of Commons that British paratroops were being flown to
                Jordan at the request of King Hussein.

                July 26. Prince Charles was named Prince of Wales by
                his mother, Queen Elizabeth II.

                October 20. British troops began to withdraw from Jor-
                dan.

                October 24. Two Comet IV jet airliners of British Over-
                seas Airways completed the first transatlantic crossings
                by commercial jet airliners.

                October 30. The United States and Britain announced
                suspension of nuclear tests, effective October 31, for
                at least one year, unless the U.S.S.R. continued its pre-
                sent series of tests.

1959   February 19. Prime Minister Macmillan, Greek Premier
                Karamanlis, Turkish Premier Menderes, Greek Cypriot
                leader Archbishop Makarios and Turkish Cypriot leader
                Kutchak signed an agreement in London to constitute
                Cyprus an independent republic.

February 28. The Government signed a financial agreement with the United Arab Republic in Cairo, ending the dispute arising from 1956 nationalization of the Suez Canal.

October 8. Prime Minister Macmillan's Conservative Party won an overwhelming victory in parliamentary elections.

November 20. The Ministers of Britain, Sweden, Norway, Denmark, Switzerland and Portugal initialed an agreement to form the European Trade Association (the Outer Seven) in Stockholm.

1960   April 8. The House of Commons unanimously passed a resolution deploring South Africa's racial policies.

May 6. Princess Margaret and Anthony Armstrong-Jones were married in Westminster Abbey.

May 15. Prime Minister Macmillan arrived in Paris for a Summit Conference. When the Conference collapsed, Macmillan held separate meetings with de Gaulle, Krushchev and Eisenhower, trying to continue the meeting.

October 21. First nuclear-powered submarine, the Dreadnought, was launched at Barrow-in-Furness.

1961   June 19. Kuwait announced termination of its protective treaty with Britain, replacing it with an agreement pledging British military aid when requested.

July 25. Chancellor of the Exchequer Selwyn Lloyd, announced stringent fiscal measures to strengthen the economy.

August 3. The House of Commons approved the Government's decision to seek membership in the European Economic Community (the Common Market).

December 27. The Government announced dispatch of naval vessels to the Persian Gulf to forestall seizure of Kuwait by Iraq.

1962   April 10. Britain and the United States issued a joint
            statement, expressing the hope that the U.S.S.R. would
            accept "international verification" of the nuclear test ban
            treaty, but declaring that they would resume atmospheric
            testing in the absence of a treaty.

            April 18. The law, limiting immigration into Great
            Britain from other Commonwealth countries, was en-
            acted.

            April 26. The British satellite, Ariel, was launched into
            orbit by United States' rockets from Cape Canaveral,
            Florida.

1963   January 18. Hugh Gaitskell, leader of the Labor Party,
            died.

            January 29. The Government was informed by the Euro-
            pean Economic Community that negotiations for British
            membership were suspended.

            April 6. The Government signed an agreement with the
            United States to buy at a future date Polaris missiles for
            the British nuclear submarine fleet.

            June 4. John Profumo resigned as Secretary of State for
            War after admitting that he had lied to Parliament in
            denying that he had committed personal improprieties
            with Christine Keeler, a 21-year old model.

            June 17. The Macmillan Government won a narrow vote
            of confidence after a House of Commons' debate on the
            Profumo affair.

            September 26. Lord Denning issued a report on the Pro-
            fumo affair, stating that British security interests had
            not been impaired, but the government was criticized for
            mishandling the affair.

            October 18. Harold Macmillan resigned as Prime Minis-
            ter. Queen Elizabeth II asked the Earl of Home, later
            Sir Alec Douglas Home, to take the office of Prime Minis-
            ter.

            December 6. Christine Keeler was sentenced to nine
            months' imprisonment on perjury and conspiracy charges.

1964   February. The Government announced agreement with
                France to construct a railroad tunnel under the English
                Channel.

                October 15. The Labor Party won the general election
                with a narrow majority of four seats in House of Com-
                mons. Harold Wilson became Prime Minister on October
                16.

1965   January 24. Former Prime Minister and World War II
                leader, Winston Churchill, died in London. The funeral
                was held January 30 and was attended by representatives
                and some leaders of 112 nations.

                April 30. The Labor Government announced its plans to
                re-nationalize the steel industry.

                July 28. Edward Heath replaced Sir Alec Douglas Home,
                who had resigned on July 22, as leader of the Conserva-
                tive Party.

                September 10. The Bank of England announced new ar-
                rangements with ten nations to bolster the pound.

                November 11. The Government denounced Rhodesia's
                uni-lateral declaration of independence. Prime Minister
                Wilson applied economic sanctions, calling the move
                illegal.

                December 17. The Government imposed an oil embargo
                on Rhodesia.

1966   February 22. The Government announced its decision to
                reduce its overseas armed forces by one-third.

                March 5. Ghana resumed diplomatic relations with
                Britain. They had been broken off by former Ghanian
                President Nkrumah over Britain's refusal to use armed
                force in Rhodesian dispute.

                March 31. The Labor Government of Prime Minister
                Harold Wilson won a sweeping electoral victory with a
                97-seat majority.

                July 20. Prime Minister Wilson made a strong effort to
                stabilize the nation's currency by calling for a 6-month

halt in scheduled wage increases, cutting travel expenses for British overseas tourists and promising lower foreign expenditures.

July 25. The House of Commons voted to nationalize the steel industry within 12 months.

October 4. The Cabinet made the wage and price freeze mandatory through the end of the year.

November 14. Prince Charles turned 18 and succeeded his father, Prince Philip, as prospective regent.

December 2-4. Prime Minister Wilson and Rhodesian Prime Minister, Ian Smith, conferred on a cruiser off Gibraltar in an unsuccessful effort to settle the crisis created by Rhodesian independence.

December 8. The Government urged the United Nations Security Council to apply economic sanctions against the export of 12 key products to Rhodesia.

December 20. Prime Minister Wilson withdrew all settlement offers to Rhodesia, indicating that the Country's legal independence must await African majority rule.

1967   March 26-30. The beaches of southern England were reported polluted by tons of crude oil from the tanker, Torrey Canyon, which had gone aground and broke up on March 18.

April 17. The Conservatives made big gains in local elections in England and Wales.

May 10. Britain formally applied for membership in the European Economic Community after many preliminary travels by Prime Minister Wilson.

September 20. Queen Elizabeth II christened the Queen Elizabeth II, Cunard luxury liner, at Clydebank, Scotland.

November 18. The pound was devalued 14.3% from $2.80 to $2.40 in order to overcome the economic crisis. The Labor Government won a vote of confidence on this issue on November 22.

1968

January 16. Prime Minister Wilson announced drastic cuts in domestic and defense spending in order to assure that devaluation would work.

March 1. Immigration of British subjects of Asian ancestry into Britain was sharply limited.

March 12. Mauritius became independent from Britain.

March 15. The gold market in London was closed until April 1 as the rush to purchase gold mounted.

July 1. Britain, the United States, the Soviet Union and 58 non-nuclear nations signed a nuclear non-proliferation treaty.

September 27. The French, under President de Gaulle, vetoed British entry into the Common Market for the third time.

December 29. Britain's Cunard Line stated that it would delay taking possession of the new liner, Queen Elizabeth II, until the builders of the vessel corrected deficiencies.

1969

January 4. In Londonderry, Northern Ireland, 136 persons were injured as Protestants attacked marching University students.

March 19. British paratroopers occupied the Caribbean island of Anguilla, ending its claim to independence.

April 6. A four-man British expedition reached the North Pole after a 14-month, 1,300 mile trek by dogsled.

July 1. Queen Elizabeth II invested her 20-year old son, Prince Charles, as the 21st Prince of Wales in ceremonies at Caernarvon Castle in Wales.

August 15. Britain began airlifting troops to Northern Ireland as violence between Catholics and Protestants spread.

September 15. The Board of Trade released figures indicating that during August the nation had a surplus in its international trade for the first time in the last two years.

December 2. The European Economic Community agreed
to open negotiations on British membership in 1970.

1970

January 1. Britain dropped the age of legal capacity from
21 to 18.

February 3. British philosopher, Bertrand Russell, died
in Wales at the age of 97.

March 1. Rhodesia formally severed ties with the British
Crown and proclaimed itself a Republic.

June 4. The Pacific island Kingdom of Tonga was proclaimed an independent nation after 70 years as a British
protectorate.

June 14. The Conservative Party won an upset victory in
the general elections. Edward Heath, Conservative
Party leader, replaced Harold Wilson as Prime Minister.

July 15. The British ports were closed down in the first
national strike since 1926.

1971

Jaunuary 12. Workers staged a one-day strike protesting
proposed industrial regulations.

January 20. Postal workers began the first nationwide
postal strike. It ended on March 8.

February 15. A decimal currency system was adopted.

May 13. Britain and the European Economic Community
(EEC) announced agreement on major issues regarding
the membership of the United Kingdom.

July 7. The government issued a White Paper urging public approval of EEC membership.

August 5. Parliament enacted the Conservative Government's labor relations bill.

August 21. The government announced it would investigate
charges that its troops had beaten and terrorized political
prisoners in Northern Ireland as a result of the conflict
between Catholics and Protestants.

September 24. The government ordered permanent expulsion of 105 Soviet representatives in Britain charging them with espionage activities.

October 4. The Labour Party Conference voted to oppose EEC entry on existing terms.

October 13. British troops tried to curb the arms flow into Northern Ireland by blowing up roads from Ireland to Ulster.

October 15. Parliament passed legislation curbing non-white immigration into England.

October 18. Conservative Government released its members of Parliament to vote as they chose on the EEC issue.

October 28. Parliament approved plans for British membership in the EEC.

1972

February 2. The British Embassy in Dublin was burned during protests over the killing of thirteen civilians in Londonderry.

February 4. The government recognized Bangladesh, which in turn announced that it would seek Commonwealth membership.

February 17. The House of Commons passed a bill adapting British law to EEC regulations.

February 28. The coal miners returned to work ending a seven-week strike that crippled industry and forced large-scale power cuts.

March 24. Prime Minister Heath announced his intention to impose direct rule on Northern Ireland and suspend its Parliament. William Whitelaw was named Secretary of State for Northern Ireland.

March 30. The House of Commons adopted an enabling bill for direct rule in Northern Ireland.

June 23. The Treasury announced it was permitting the pound sterling to float in the international money markets indefinitely.

July 8. Home Secretary Reginald Maulding resigned because of his past connection with a bankrupt firm.

July 28. Dockworkers struck after they rejected proposals
to ease the unemployment situation casued by containeri-
zation.

August 1. A White Paper proposed the first major reforms
in 24 years in socialized medicine.

August 16. The dock workers' union voted to end the 20-
day strike although militants protested and indicated that
they would not accept the union's decision.

October 4. The Labour Party annual meeting called for the
renegotiation of the terms for British entrance into the
EEC.

October 21. Present and prospective members of the EEC
held a summit meeting at which they approved the prin-
ciple of an economic, monetary and diplomatic union by
1980.

November 6. Prime Minister Heath announced the institution of a 90-day freeze on prices, wages, rents and di-
vidends as a means of curbing inflation.

1973   January 17. Prime Minister Heath announced some of the
aspects of Stage Two of the anti-inflation program.

February 27-March 1. Crippling strikes occurred in Britain. The workers were demanding greater wage increases
than those provided by Stage Two.

April 2. Stage Two sent into effect. The Pay Board was
given power to rule on wage claims. The price freeze continued until April 29 when the Price Commission began to
operate.

May 22-24. Lord Lambton and Lord Jellicoe, respectively
Defense undersecretary for the Royal Air Force and leader
of the House of Lords resigned when it became public knowledge that they had associated with prostitutes.

June 5. Prime Minister Heath announced the new Cabinet
appointments replacing Lord Lambton and Lord Jellicoe.

Anthony Kershaw was made Defense undersecretary for
the Royal Air Force, and Lord Windlesham became Lord
Privy Seal.

DOCUMENTS

The documents have been selected in order to illustrate the developments in English history since 1485. The Magna Charta has been included because of the concepts contained within it which have formed a basis for the rights of all Englishmen. All other materials included were chosen as a means of indicating the subtle methods by which English social, cultural and political life has changed. Many aspects of domestic, foreign, and colonial and imperial affairs are represented in the documents. Sources are listed at the beginning of each introdution. Students who wish to consult additional documentary matter should utilize the works listed in the Source Materials section of the Bibliography.

THE MAGNA CHARTA, June 15, 1215

Source: Guy C. Lee, ed. Source-Book of English History. Leading Documents. . . . (New York: H. Holt and Company, 1900), pp. 169-178.

Although the Magna Charta was signed by King John in 1215, before the period covered in this chronology, it is important because of the role it has come to play in the development of the rights of Englishmen. The charter was originally intended to guarantee the rights of the nobility but was eventually reinterpreted to guarantee the rights of all Englishmen.

THE MAGNA CHARTA

*   *   *

1. In the first place we [John] have granted to God, and by this our present charter confirmed, for us and our heirs forever, that the English church shall be free, and shall hold its rights entire and its liberties uninjured; and we will that it thus be observed; which is shown by this, that the freedom of elections, which is considered to be most important and especially necessary to the English church, we, of our pure and spontaneous will, granted, and by our charter confirmed, before the contest between us and our barons had arisen; and obtained a confirmation of it by the lord Pope Innocent III.; which we will observe and which we will shall be observed in good faith by our heirs forever.

We have granted moreover to all free men of our kingdom for us and our heirs forever all the liberties written below, to be had and holden by themselves and their heirs from us and our heirs.

2. If any of our earls or barons, or others holding from us in chief by military service shall have died, and when he has died his heir shall be of full age and owe relief, he shall have his inheritance by the ancient relief; that is to say, the heir or heirs of an earl for the whole barony of an earl a hundred pounds; the heir or heirs of a baron for a whole barony a hundred pounds; the heir or heirs of a knight, for a whole knight's fee, a hundred shillings at most; and who owes less let him give less according to the ancient custom of fiefs.

3. If moreover the heir of any one of such shall be under age, and shall be in wardship, when he comes of age he shall have his inheritance without relief and without a fine.

4. The custodian of the land of such a minor heir shall not take from the land of the heir any except reasonable products, reasonable customary payments, and reasonable services, and this without destruction or waste of men or of property; and if we shall have committed the custody of the land of any such a one to the sheriff or to any other who is to be responsible to us for its proceeds, and that man shall have caused destruction or waste from his custody we will recover damages

from him, and the land shall be committed to two legal and discreet men of that fief, who shall be responsible for its proceeds to us or to him to whom we have assigned them; and if we shall have given or sold to any one the custody of any such land, and he has caused destruction or waste there, he shall lose that custody, and it shall be handed over to two legal and discreet men of that fief who shall be in like manner responsible to us as is said above.

5. The custodian moreover, so long as he shall have the custody of the land, must keep up the houses, parks, warrens, fish ponds, mills, and other things pertaining to the land, from the proceeds of the land itself; and he must return to the heir, when he has come to full age, all his land, furnished with ploughs and implements of husbandry according as the time of wainage requires and as the proceeds of the land are able reasonably to sustain.

6. Heirs shall be married without disparity, so nevertheless that before the marriage is contracted, it shall be announced to the relatives by blood of the heir himself.

*   *   *

10. If any one has taken anything from the Jews, by way of a loan, more or less, and dies before that debt is paid, the debt shall not draw interest so long as the heir is under age, from whomsoever he holds; and if that debt falls into our hands, we will take nothing except the chattel contained in the agreement.

11. And if any one dies leaving a debt owing to the Jews, his wife shall have her dowry, and shall pay nothing of that debt; and if there remain minor children of the dead man, necessaries shall be provided for them corresponding to the holding of the dead man; and from the remainder shall be paid the debt, the service of the lords being retained. In the same way debts are to be treated which are owed to others than the Jews.

12. No scutage or aid shall be imposed in our kingdom except by the common council of our kingdom, except for the ransoming of our body, for the making of our oldest son a knight, and for once marrying our oldest daughter, and for these purposes it shall be only a reasonable aid; in the same way it shall be done concerning the aids of the city of London.

13. And the city of London shall have all its ancient liberties and free customs, as well by land as by water. Moreover, we will and grant that all other cities and boroughs and villages and ports shall have all their liberties and free customs.

14. And for holding a common council of the kingdom concerning the assessment of an aid otherwise than in the three cases mentioned above, or concerning the assessment of a scutage, we shall cause to be summoned the archbishops, bishops, abbots, earls, and greater barons by our letters under seal; and besides we shall cause to be summoned generally, by our sheriffs and bailiffs, all those who hold from us in chief, for a certain day, that is at the end of forty days at least, and for a certain place; and in all the letters of that summons, we will express

the cause of the summons and when the summons has thus been given
the business shall proceed on the appointed day, on the advice of those
who shall be present, even if not all of those who were summoned have
come.

*   *   *

38. No bailiff for the future shall place anyone to his law on his simple
affirmation, without credible witnesses brought for this purpose.

39. No free man shall be taken or imprisoned or dispossessed, or
outlawed, or banished, or in any way destroyed, nor will we go upon him,
nor send upon him, except by the legal judgment of his peers or by the
law of the land.

40. To no one will we sell, to no one will we deny, or delay right
or justice.

41. All merchants shall be safe and secure in going out from England
and coming into England and in remaining and going through England,
as well by land as by water, for buying and selling, free from all evil
tolls, by the ancient and rightful customs, except in time of war, and if
they are of a land at war with us; and if such are found in our land at
the beginning of war, they shall be attached without injury to their bodies
or goods, until it shall be known from us or from our principal justiciar
in what way the merchants of our land are treated who shall be then found
in the country which is at war with us; and if ours are safe there, the
others shall be safe in our land.

*   *   *

52. If anyone shall have been dispossessed or removed by us without
legal judgment of his peers, from his lands, castles, franchises, or his
right we will restore them to him immediately; and if contention arises
about this, then it shall be done according to the judgment of the twenty-
five barons, of whom mention is made below concerning the security of
the peace. Concerning all those things, however, from which anyone has
been removed or of which he has been deprived without legal judgment
of his peers by King Henry our father, or by King Richard our brother,
which we have in our hand, or which others hold, and which is our duty
to guarantee, we shall have respite till the usual term of crusaders;
excepting those things about which the suit has been begun or the in-
quisition made by our writ before our assumption of the cross; when,
however, we shall return from our journey, or if by chance we desist
from the journey, we will immediately show full justice in regard to
them.

*   *   *

THE SIX ARTICLES, MAY 1539

Source: Guy C. Lee, ed. Source-Book of English History. Leading Documents... (New York: H. Holt and Company, 1900) pp. 267-268.

> This Act was passed as part of the English
> Reformation. Henry VIII was determined to
> maintain the basic doctrine of the Catholic
> Church. However, he was as determined to
> prevent the development of diverse opinions
> within the Church. The Six Articles estab-
> lishes the orthodoxy which was to be followed
> by the Anglican Church.

1539   CHAPTER 14

AN ACT ABOLISHING DIVERSITY IN OPINIONS

Whereas the King's most excellant Majesty is by God's law supreme head immediately under Him of this whole Church and Congregation of England, intending the conservation of the same Church and Congregation in a true, sincere, and uniform doctrine of Christ's Religion, calling also to His blessed and most gracious remembrance as well the great and quiet assurance, prosperous increase, and other innumerable commodities which have ever ensued, come, and followed of concord, agreement, and unity in opinions, as also the manifold perils, danger, and inconveniences, which have heretofore in many places and regions grown, sprung, and arisen of the diversities of minds and opinions, especially of matters of Christian Religion; and therefore desiring that such an unity might and should be charitably established in all things touching and concerning the same, as the same so being established might chiefly be to the honor of Almighty God, the very Author and Fountain of all true unity and sincere concord, and consequently redowned to the common-wealth of this his highness' most noble realm, and of all his loving subjects and other residents and inhabitants of or in the same; hath therefore caused and commanded this his most high Court of Parliament, for sundry and many urgent causes and considerations, to be at this time summoned, and also a synod and convocation of all the archbishops, bishops, and other learned men of the clergy of this his realm, to be in like manner assembled; and forasmuch as in the said Parliament, synod, and convocation there were certain articles, matters, and questions appointed and set forth touching Christian Religion, that is to say; First, whether in the most blessed Sacrament of the Altar remaineth after the consecration of the substance of bread and wine or no; Secondly, whether it be necessary by God's law that all men should be communicate with both

kinds or no; Thirdly, whether priests, that is to say men dedicated to God
by priesthood, may by the law of God marry after or no: Fourthly, whether
vow of chastity or widowhood made to God advisedly by man or woman be
by the law of God to be observed or no; Fifthly, whether private Masses
stand with the law of God and be to be used and continued in the Church and
Congregation of England as things whereby good Christian people may and
do receive both Godly consolation and wholesome benefits or no; Sixthly,
whether auricular confession is necessary to be retained, continued, used,
and frequented in the Church or no; the King's most Royal Majesty, most
prudently pondering and considering that by occasion of variable and sundry
opinions and judgments of the said Articles, great discord and variance
hath arisen as well amongst the clergy of this his realm, as amongst a
great number of vulgar people, his loving subjects of the same, and being
in a full hope and trust that a full and perfect resolution of the said Articles
should make a perfect concord and unity generally amongst all his loving
and obedient subjects; of his most excellant goodness not only commanded
that the said Articles should deliberately and advisedly by his said archbishops, bishops, and other learned men of his clergy, be debated, argued,
and reasoned, and their opinions therein to be understood, declared, and
known, but also most graciously vouchsafed in his own princely person to
descend and come into his said high court of Parliament and Council, and
there, like a prince of most high prudence and no less learning, opened and
declared many things of high learning and great knowledge touching the said
articles, matters, and questions, for an unity to be had in the same; Where-
upon, after a great and long deliberate and advised disputation and consultation had and made concerning the said Articles, as well by the consent of
the King's Highness as by the assent of the Lords Spiritual and Temporal,
and other learned men of his clergy in their convocation, and by the consent of the Commons in this present Parliament assembled, it was, and is,
finally resolved, accorded, and agreed in manner and form following, that
is to say; First, that in the most blessed Sacrament of the Altar, by the
strength and efficacy of Christ's mighty word, it being spoken by the priest,
is present really, under the form of bread and wine, the natural body and
blood of our Saviour Jesus Christ, conceived of the Virgin Mary, and that
after the consecration there remaineth no substance of bread or wine, nor
any other substance but the substance of Christ, God and Man; Secondly,
that communion in both kinds is not necessary ad salutem by the law of God
to all persons; and that it is to be believed and not doubted of, but that in
the flesh under form of bread is the very blood, and with the blood under
form of wine is the very flesh, as well apart as though they were both together; Thirdly, that priests after the order of priesthood received, as before, may not marry by the law of God; Fourthly, that vows of chastity or
widowhood by man or woman made to God advisedly ought to be observed by
the law of God, and that it exempts them from other liberties of Christian
people, which, without that, they might enjoy; Fifthly, that it is meet and
necessary that private Masses be continued and admitted in this the King's

English Church and Congregation, as whereby good Christian people order-
ing themselves accordingly do receive both Godly and goodly consolations
and benefits, and it is agreeable also to God's law; Sixthly, that auricular
confession is expedient and necessary to be retained and continued, used
and frequented, in the Church of God;...

MANDATE FOR CHURCH SERVICES IN ENGLISH, 1545

Source: Guy C. Lee, ed., Source-Book of English History. Leading Documents...(New York: H. Holt and Company, 1900) pp. 271-272.

> This Mandate broke the custom of conducting
> the services in Latin and required that they be in
> English. Consequently the communicants were
> able to better understand the services. All ser-
> vices since have been conducted in English.

A MANDATE FOR PUBLISHING AND USING THE PRAYERS IN THE ENGLISH TONGUE

Most reverend father in God, right trusty and right well-beloved, we greet you well, and let you wit, that calling to our remembrance the miserable state of all Christendom, being at this present, besides all other troubles, so plagued with most cruel wars, hatred, and dissensions, as no place of the same almost (being the whole reduced to a very narrow corner) remaineth in good peace, agreement, and concord; the help and remedy whereof far exceeding the power of any man, must be called for of Him who only is able to grant our petitions, and never forsaketh nor repelleth any that firmly believe and faithfully call on him; unto whom also the example of Scripture encourageth us, in all these and other our troubles and necessities, to fly and to cry for aid and succour; being therefore resolved to have continually from henceforth general processions, in all cities, towns, churches, and parishes in this our realm, said and sung, with such reverence and devotion as appertaineth. Forasmuch as heretofore the people, partly for lack of good instruction and calling, and partly for that they understood no part of such prayers or suffrages as were used to be sung and said, have used to come very slackly to the procession, when the same have been commanded heretofore; we have set forth certain godly prayers and suffrages in our native English tongue, which we send you herewith, signifying unto you, that for the special trust and confidence we have of your godly mind, and earnest desire, to the setting forward of the glory of God, and the true worshipping of his most holy name, within that province committed by us unto you, we have sent unto you these suffrages, not to be for a month or two observed, and after slenderly considered, as other our injunctions have, to our no little marvel, been used; but to the intent that as well the same, as other our injunctions, may be earnestly set forth by preaching good exhortations and otherwise to the people, in such sort as they feeling the godly taste thereof, may godly and joyously, with thanks, receive, embrace, and frequent the same, as appertaineth. Wherefore we will and command you, as you will answer unto us for the contrary, not

only to cause these prayers and suffrages aforesaid to be published, frequented, and openly used in all towns, churches, villages, and parishes of
your own diocess, but also to signify this our pleasure unto all other bishops of your province, willing and commanding them in our name, and by
virtue hereof, to do and execute the same accordingly. Unto whose proceedings, in the execution of this our commandment, we will that you have
a special respect, and make report unto us, if any shall not with good dex-
terity accomplish the same; not failing, as our special trust is in you.

At St. James's, Junii -- Regni 36. Directed to
the Archbishop of Canterbury

THE MILLENARY PETITION, APRIL 1603.

Source: Guy C. Lee, ed. Source-Book of English History. Leading Documents... (New York: H. Holt and Company, 1900) pp. 338-341.

> James I was presented with this document
> by the Puritan clergymen as he was travelling
> to London to claim his throne. The petition
> requested a complete reform of the Church in-
> cluding the service; the selection of ministers;
> the holding of offices; church discipline and
> correction of other abuses. As a result of
> these requests, the Hampton Court Conference
> took place in which James indicated his de-
> termination to maintain the Anglican Church
> with its Episcopal hierarchy.

THE HUMBLE PETITION OF THE MINISTERS OF THE CHURCH OF ENGLAND DESIRING REFORMATION OF CERTAIN CEREMONIES AND ABUSES OF THE CHURCH

To the most Christian and excellent prince, our gracious and dread Sovereign, James, by the grace of God, etc., we, the ministers of the Church of England that desire reformation, wish a long, prosperous and happy reign over us in this life, and in the next everlasting salvation.

Most gracious and dread Sovereign, seeing it hath pleased the Divine Majesty, to the great comfort of all good Christians, to advance your Highness, according to your just title, to the peaceable government of this church and commonwealth of England, we, the ministers of the gospel in this land, neither as factious men affecting a popular parity in the church, nor as schismatics aiming at the dissolution of the state ecclesiastical, but as the faithful servants of Christ and loyal subjects of your Majesty's, desiring and longing for the redress of divers abuses of the church, could do no less in our obedience to God, service to your Majesty, love to his church, than acquaint your princely Majesty with our particular griefs. For, as your princely pen writeth, the King as a good physician must first know what peccant humours his patient naturally is most subject unto before he can begin his cure. And although divers of us that sue for refor-mation have formerly in respect of the times subscribed to the book, some upon protestation, some upon exposition given them, some with condition, rather than the church should have been deprived of their labour and min-istry, yet now we, to the number of more than a thousand of your Majesty's subjects and ministers, all groaning as under a common burthen of human rites and ceremonies, do with one joint consent humble ourselves at your

Majesty's feet, to be eased and relieved in this behalf. Our humble suit
then unto your Majesty is, that of these offences following, some may be
removed, some amended, some qualified:

I. In the church service: -- That the cross in baptism, interrogatories
ministered to infants, confirmation, as superfluous, may be taken away.
Baptism not to be ministered by women, and so explained. The cap and
surplice not urged. That examination may go before the communion. That
it be ministered with a sermon. That divers terms of priests and absolu-
tion and some other used, with the ring in marriage, and other such like in
the book may be corrected. The longsomeness of service abridged.
Church songs and music moderated to better edification. That the Lord's
day be not profaned: the rest upon holidays not so strictly urged. That
there be an uniformity of doctrine prescribed. No popish opinion to be any
more taught or defended: no ministers charged to teach their people to
bow at the name of Jesus. That the canonical scriptures only be read in
the church.

II. Concerning church ministers: -- That none hereafter be admitted
into the ministry but able and sufficient men, and those to preach diligently, and especially upon the Lord's day. That such as be already entered
and cannot preach may either be removed and some charitable course tak-
en with them for their relief, or else to be forced, according to the value
of their livings, to maintain preachers. That nonresidency be not permitted.
That King Edward's statute [5 & 6 E. VI. 12] for the lawfulness of ministers' marriage be revived. That ministers be not urged to subscribe but
according to the law to the articles of religion and the King's supremacy
only.

III. For church living and maintenance: -- That bishops leave their
commendams, some holding prebends, some parsonages, some vicarages,
with their bishoprics. That double-beneficed men be not suffered to hold
some two, some three benefices with cure, and some two, three or four
dignities besides. That impropriations annexed to bishoprics and colleges
be demised only to the preachers' incumbents for the old rent. That the
impropriations of layman's fees may be charged with a sixth or seventh
party of the worth, to the maintenance of the preaching minister.

IV. For church discipline: -- That the discipline and excommunication may be administered according to Christ's own institution, or at least
that enormities may be redressed; as, namely, that excommunication come
not forth under the name of lay persons, chancellors, officials, etc. That
men be not excommunicated for trifles and twelve-penny matters: that
none be excommunicated without the consent of his pastor. That the offices
be not suffered to extort unreasonable fees. That none having jurisdiction
or registers' places put out the same to farm. That divers popish canons
(as for restraint of marriage at certain times) be reversed. That the longsomeness of suits in ecclesiastical courts, which hang sometimes two,
three, four, five, six or seven years, may be restrained. That the oath ex
officio, whereby men are forced to accuse themselves, be more sparingly

used. That licences for marriage without banns asked be more cautiously granted.

These, with such other abuses yet remaining and practised in the Church of England, we are able to show not to be agreeable to the Scriptures, if it shall please your Highness further to hear us, or more at large by writing to be informed, or by conference among the learned to be resolved. And yet we doubt not but that without any further process your Majesty (of whose Christian judgment we have received so good a taste already) is able of yourself to judge of the equity of this cause. God, we trust, hath appointed your Highness our physician to heal these diseases. And we say with Mordecai to Hester, "Who knoweth whether you are come to the kingdom for such a time?" [Esth. iv. 14]. Thus your Majesty shall do that which we are persuaded shall be acceptable to God, honourable to your Majesty in all succeeding ages, profitable to his church, which shall be no more suspended, silenced, disgraced, imprisoned for men's traditions, and prejudicial to none but to those that seek their own quiet, credit and profit in the world. Thus with all dutiful submission referring ourselves to your Majesty's pleasure for your gracious answer as God shall direct you, we most humbly recommend your Highness to the Divine Majesty, whom we beseech for Christ his sake to dispose your royal heart to do herein what shall be to his glory, the good of his church, and your endless comfort.

Your Majesty's most humble subjects, the ministers of the gospel, that desire, not a disorderly innovation, but a due and godly reformation.

THE PETITION OF RIGHT, June 7, 1628

Source: Guy C. Lee, ed. Source-Book of English History. Leading Documents... (New York: H. Holt and Company, 1900) pp. 348-352.

Charles I, who had come to the throne in
1625 found that Parliament was determined to
compel him to guarantee certain rights for
all Englishmen. They insisted in this Petition that the King agree to desist from forced
loans including imprisonment of those who resisted; to stop the practice of quartering
soldiers in private residences; and to end the
use of martial law for punishment of those
who resisted the King. Charles was eventually
forced to give his assent to these demands.

THE PETITION EXHIBITED TO HIS MAJESTY BY THE LORDS SPIR-
ITUAL AND TEMPORAL, AND COMMONS IN THIS PRESENT
PARLIAMENT ASSEMBLED, CONCERNING DIVERS RIGHTS
AND LIBERTIES OF THE SUBJECTS, WITH THE KING'S MAJ-
ESTY'S ROYAL ANSWER THEREUNTO IN FULL PARLIAMENT

To the King's Most Excellent Majesty.

* * * * * * * *

[The Lords Spiritual and Temporal, and Commons in Parliament]
do...humbly pray your Most Excellent Majesty, that no man hereafter be
compelled to make or yield any gift, loan, benevolence, tax, or such like
charge, without common consent by Act of Parliament; and that none be
called to take answer, or take such oath, or to give attendance, or be
charged or otherwise molested or disquieted concerning the same, or for
refusal thereof; and that no freeman, in any such manner as is before-men-
tioned, be imprisoned or detained; and that your Majesty will be pleased to
remove the said soldiers and mariners, and that your people may not be
so burdened in time to come; and that the foresaid commissions for proceeding by martial law, may be revoked and annulled; and that hereafter
no commissions of like nature may issue forth to any person or persons
whatsoever, to be executed as aforesaid, lest by colour of them any of
your Majesty's subjects be destroyed or put to death, contrary to the laws
and franchise of the land.

All which they most humbly pray of your Most Excellent Majesty, as
their rights and liberties according to the laws and statutes of this realm:
and that your Majesty would also vouchsafe to declare, that the awards,

doings, and proceedings to the prejudice of your people, in any of the premises, shall not be drawn hereafter into consequence or example: and that
your Majesty would be also graciously pleased, for the further comfort and
safety of your people, to declare your royal will and pleasure, that in the
things aforesaid all your officers and ministers shall serve you, according to the laws and statutes of this realm, as they tender the honour of
your Majesty, and the prosperity of this kingdom.

THE FIRST WRIT OF SHIP MONEY, October 20, 1634

Source: Guy C. Lee, ed. Source-Book of English History. Leading Documents...(New York: H. Holt and Company, 1900) pp 352-355.

> After Charles I had been forced to accept
> the Petition of Right, he became determined
> to rule without Parliament. When he found
> that his financial resources were not sufficient
> he had investigations made as to the rights
> of the monarch during the medieval period.
> He revived an old law requiring coastal ci-
> ties and counties to supply ships for the
> royal navy. He then extended it to the in-
> land areas as well. Since the smaller sea-
> coast towns and the inland cities could not
> send ships, he required them to pay a money
> equivalent. There was a certain amount of
> opposition based on the fact that the King was
> using the money for his own purposes rather
> than the navy. John Hampden refused to pay
> his assessment and was brought before the
> Court of Exchequer where the judges gave a
> verdict in favor of the King. This indicated
> their subserviency to the Crown.

To the Mayor, commonalty, and citizens of our city of London, and to
the sheriffs of the same city, and good men in the siad city and in the liberties, and members of the same, greeting: Because we are given to under-
stand that certain thieves, pirates, and robbers of the sea, as well Turks,
enemies of the Christian name, as others, being gathered together, wicked-
ly taking by force and spoiling the ships, and goods, and merchandises, not
only of our subjects, but also the subjects of our friends in the sea, which
hath been accustomed anciently to be defended by the English nation, and
the same, at their pleasure, have carried away, delivering the men in the
same into miserable captivity: and forasmuch as we see them daily pre-
paring all manner of shipping farther to molest our merchants, and to
grieve the kingdom, unless remedy be not sooner applied, and their endeavours be not more manly met withal; also the dangers considered which,
on every side, in these times of war do hang over our heads, that it be-
hoveth us and our subjects to hasten the defence of the sea and kingdom
with all expedition or speed that we can; we willing by the help of God
chiefly to provide for the defence of the kingdom, safeguard of the sea, security of our subjects, safe conduct of ships and merchandises to our king-

dom of England coming, and from the same kingdom to foreign parts passing; forasmuch as we, and our progenitors, Kings of England, have been

always heretofore masters of the aforesaid sea, and it would be very irk-
some unto us if that princely honour in our times should be lost or in any
thing diminished. (And although that charge of defence which concerneth
all men ought to be supported by all, as by the laws and customs of the
kingdom of England hath been accustomed to be done: notwithstanding we
considering that you constituted in the sea-coasts, to whom by sea as well
great dangers are imminent, and who by the same do get more plentiful
gains for the defence of the sea, and conservation of our princely honour
in that behalf, according to the duty of your allegiance against such attempts, are chiefly bound to set to your helping hand; we command firmly,
enjoining you the aforesaid Mayor, commonalty and citizens, and sheriffs
of the said city, and the good men in the same city and in the liberties, and
members of the same, in the faith and allegiance wherein you are bound
unto us, and as you do love us and our honour, and under the forfeiture of
all which you can forfeit to us, that you cause to be prepared and brought
to the port of Portsmouth, before the first day of March now next ensuing,
one ship of war of the burden of nine hundred tons, with three hundred and
fifty men at the least, as well expert masters, as very able and skilful
mariners; one other ship of war of the burden of eight hundred tons, with
two hundred and sixty men at the least, as well skilful masters, as very
able and expert mariners: four other ships of war, every of them of the
burden of five hundred tons, and every of them with two hundred men at
the least, as well expert masters, as very able and skilful mariners: and
one other ship of war of the burden of three hundred tons, with a hundred
and fifty men, as well expert masters, as very able and skilful mariners:
and also every of the said ships with ordnance, as well greater as lesser,
gunpowder, and spears and weapons, and other necessary arms sufficient
for war, and with double tackling, and with victuals, until the said first of
March, competent for so many men; and from that time, for twenty-six
weeks, at your charges, as well in victuals as men's wages, and other
things necessary for war, during that time, upon defence of the sea in our
service, in command of the admiral of the sea, to whom we shall commit
the custody of the sea, before the aforesaid first day of March, and as he,
on our behalf, shall command them to continue; so that they may be there
the same day, at the farthest, to go from thence with our ships, and the
ships of other faithful subjects, for the safeguard of the sea, and defence
of you and yours, and repulse and vanquishing of whomsoever busying
themselves to molest or trouble upon the sea our merchants, and other
subjects, and faithful people coming into our dominions for cause of mer-
chandise, or from thence returning to their own countries. Also we have
assigned you, the aforesaid Mayor and Aldermen of the city aforesaid, or
any thirteen, or more of you, within thirteen days after the receipt of this
writ to assess all men in the said city, and in the liberties and members
of the same, and the landholders in the same, not having a ship, or any

part of the aforesaid ships, not serving in the same, to contribute to the expenses, about the necessary provision of the premises; and to assess and lay upon the aforesaid city, with the liberties and members thereof, viz. upon every of them according to their estate and substances, and the portion assessed upon them; and to nominate and appoint collectors in this behalf. Also we have assigned you, the aforesaid Mayor, and also the Sheriffs of the city aforesaid, to levy the portions so as aforesaid assessed upon the aforesaid men and landholders, and every of them in the aforesaid city, with the liberties and members of the same, by distress and other due means; and to commit to prison all those whom you shall find rebellious and contrary in the premises, there to remain until we shall give further order for their delivery. And moreover we command you, that about the premises you diligently attend, and do, and execute those things with effect, upon peril that shall fall thereon: but we will not, that under colour of our aforesaid command, more should be levied of the said men than shall suffice for the necessary expenses of the premises; or that any who have levied money for contribution to raise the aforesaid charges, should by him detain the same, or any part thereof; or should presume, by any manner of colour, to appropriate the same to other uses; willing, that if more than may be sufficient shall be collected, the same may be paid out among the contributors, for the rate of the part to them belonging.

Witness myself, at Westminster the twentieth day
of October, in the tenth year of our reign.

DECLARATION OF THE ARMY, JUNE 14, 1647

Source: William Heller and Godfrey Davies, eds. The Leveller Tracts,
1647-1653. (New York: Columbia University Press, 1944) pp. 52-63.

> The Army which had been developed and trained
> under the guidelines set down by Oliver Cromwell
> had done quite well in fighting the forces loyal to
> King Charles I. They were determined that their
> struggle not have been made in vain. They re-
> commended the reorganization of the government
> and the methods for regulation of the state.

A DECLARATION, OR REPRESENTATION FROM HIS EXCELLENCY, SIR THOMAS FAIRFAX, AND OF THE ARMY UNDER HIS COMMAND, HUMBLY TENDERED TO THE PARLIAMENT

That we may no longer be the dissatisfaction of our friends, the subject of our enemies malice (to work jealousies and misrepresentations upon) and the suspicion (if not astonishment) of many in the Kingdom, in our
late or present transactions and conduct of business; we shall in all faith-
fulness and clearness profess, and declare unto you, those things which
have of late protracted and hindered our disbanding, the present grievances
which possess our Army, and are yet unremedied, with our desires, as to
the complete settlement of the liberties and peace of the kingdom; which is
more dear unto us, or more precious in our thoughts, we having hitherto
thought all our present enjoyments (whether of life or livelihood, or near-
est relations) a price but sufficient to the purchase of so rich a blessing;
that we, and all the free born people of this Nation, may sit down in quiet
under our Vines, under the glorious administration of Justice, and righte-
ousness, and in the full possession of those Fundamental Rights and Liberties, without which we can have little hopes (as to humane considerations)
to enjoy either any comforts of life, or so much as life itself, but at the
pleasures of some men, ruling merely according to will and power.

* * *

... we shall proceed to propound such things as we do humbly desire
for the settling and securing of our own and the Kingdom's common right,
freedom, peace, and safety, as follows.

1. That the Houses may be speedily purged of such members, as for
their Delinquency, or for Corruptions, or abuse to the State, or undo Elections, ought not to sit there: whereof the late elections in Cornwall, Wales
and other parts of the Kingdom afford too many examples, to the great

prejudice of the people's freedom in the said elections.

2. That those persons, who have, in the unjust and high proceedings against the Army appeared to have the will, the confidence, credit, and power, to abuse the Parliament, and the Army, and endanger the Kingdom in carrying on such things against us (while an Army) may be some way speedily disabled from doing the like or worse to us (when disbanded and dispersed, and in the condition of private men) or to other free-born people of England in the same condition with us, and that for that purpose, the same persons may not continue in the same power (especially as our and the Kingdom's Judges in the highest trust) but may be made incapable thereof for the future.

***

3. That some determinate period of time may be set, for the continuance of this and future Parliaments, beyond which none shall continue and upon which new Writs may of course issue out, and new Elections successively take place according to the intent of the Bill for Triennial Parliaments . . . .

4. That secure provisions may be made for the continuance of future Parliaments, so as they may not be adjournable or dissolveable at the King's pleasure, or any other ways than by their own consent during their respective periods, but at those periods each Parliament to determine of course as before. This we desire may be now provided for (if it may be) so as to put it out of all dispute, for future, though we think of right, it ought not to have been otherwise before.

***

5. That some Provision may be now made for such Distribution of Elections for future Parliaments, as may stand with some Rule of Equality or Proportion, as near as may be, to render the Parliament a more equal Representative of the whole; . . . .

6. We desire, that the right and freedom of the people, to represent to the Parliament by way of humble Petition, their grievances (in such things as cannot otherwise be remedied than by Parliament) may be cleared and vindicated. That all such grievances of the people may be freely received and admitted into consideration, and put into an equitable and speedy way, to be heard, examined, and redressed (if they appear real) and that in such things for which men have remedy by law, they may be freely left to the benefit of law, and the regulated course of Justice, without interruption or check from Parliament, except in case of things done upon the exigency of War, or for the service and benefit of the Parliament and Kingdom in relation to the War, or otherwise, in due pursuance and execution of Ordinances or Orders of Parliament.

7. That the large powers, given to the Committees or Deputy Lieutenants during the late times of War and destruction, may be speedily taken into consideration, That such of these powers as appear not necessary to be continued, may be taken away, and such of them as are necessary may

be put into a regulated way, and left to as little Arbitrariness, as the nature and necessity of the things wherein they are conversant will bear.

8. We could wish that the Kingdom might both be righted and publicly satisfied in point of Accounts, for the vast sums that have been levied and paid, as also in divers other things wherein the Commonwealth may be conceived to have been wronged or abused; But we are loathe to press any thing, that may tend to lengthen out future disputes or contestations, but rather such as may tend to a speedy and general composure, and quieting of men's minds, in order to have Peace, ...

9. That (public Justice being first satisfied by some few examples to posterity out of the worst of excepted persons, and other Delinquents, having passed their Compositions) some course may be taken (by a general Act of oblivion or otherwise) whereby the seeds of future War or feuds, either to the present age, or posterity, may the better be taken away, by easing that sense of present, and satisfying those fears of future Ruin or Undoing, to persons or families, which may drive men into any desperate ways for self preservation or remedy, and by taking away the private remembrances and distinction of parties, as far as may stand with safety to the rights and Liberties we have hitherto fought for.

****

We have thus freely and clearly declared the depth and bottom of our hearts and desires in order to the Rights, Liberties and Peace of the Kingdom, wherein we appeal to all men, whether we seek any thing of advantage to ourselves or any particular party whatever, to the prejudice of the whole, and whether the things we wish and seek, do not equally concern and conduce to the good of others in common with ourselves, according to the sincerity of our desires and intentions wherein, . . . we shall wish and expect to find the unanimous concurrence of all others, who are equally concerned with us in these things, and wish well to the Public. And so trusting in the mercy and goodness of God to pass by and help any failings or infirmities of ours, in the carriage or proceedings hereupon, we shall humbly cast ourselves and the business upon his good pleasure, depending only on his presence and blessing for an happy issue to the peace and good of this poor Kingdom, in the accomplishment whereof, we desire and hope, that God will make you blessed Instruments.

June 14th 1647

By the appointment of his Excellency Sir Thomas Fairfax, with the Officers and Soldiery of his Army,

Signed,
Jo: RUSHWORTH
Secretary

THE CHARGES AGAINST CHARLES I, 1649

Source: Guy C. Lee, ed. Source-Book of English History. Leading Documents... (New York: H. Holt and Company, 1900) pp. 364-366.

> After a long civil war interspersed with
> peace negotiations during the 1640's, the
> Parliament was able to take Charles I
> prisoner and bring him to trial. The follow-
> ing charge brought against the King was part
> of a concerted campaign which led to his con-
> viction and execution in January, 1649.

THE CHARGE AGAINST THE KING

That the said Charles Stuart, being admitted King of England, and therein trusted with a limited power to govern by and according to the laws of the land, and not otherwise; and by his trust, oath, and office, being obliged to use the power committed to him for the good and benefit and liberties; yet, nevertheless, out of a wicked design to erect and uphold in himself an unlimited and tyrannical power to rule according to his will, and to overthrow the rights and liberties of the people, yea, to take away and make void the foundations thereof, and of all redress and remedy of misgovernment, which by the fundamental constitutions of this kingdom were reserved on the people's behalf in the right and power of frequent and successive Parliaments, or national meetings in Council; he, the said Charles Stuart, for accomplishment of such his designs, and for the pro- tecting of himself and his adherents in his and their wicked practices, to the same ends hath traitorously and maliciously levied war against the pre- sent Parliament, and the people therein represented, particularly upon or about the 30th day of June, in the year of our Lord 1642, at Beverly, in the County of York; and upon or about the 30th day of July in the year aforesaid in the County of the City of York; and upon or about the 24th day of August in the same year, at the County of the Town of Nottingham, where and when he set up his standard of war; and also on or about the 23rd day of October in the same year, at Edgehill or Keynton-field, in the County of Warwick; and upon or about the 30th day of November in the same year, at Brentford, in the County of Middlesex; and upon or about the 30th day of August, in the year of our Lord 1643, at the Caversham Bridge, near Read- ing, in the County of Berks; and upon or about the 30th day of October in the year last mentioned, at or upon the City of Gloucester; and upon or about the 30th day of November in the year last mentioned, at Newbury, in the County of Berks; and upon or about the 31st day of July, in the year of our Lord 1644, at Cropredy Bridge, in the County of Oxon; and upon or

about the 30th day of September in the last year mentioned, ... At which
several times and places, or most of them, and at many other places in
this land, at several other times within the years aforementioned, and in
the year of our Lord 1646, he, the said Charles Stuart, hath caused and procured many thousands of the free people of this nation to be slain; and by

divisions, parties, and insurrections within this land, by invasions from
foreign parts, endeavoured and procured by him, and by many other evil
ways and means, he, the said Charles Stuart, hath not only maintained and
carried on the said war both by land and sea, during the years beforemen-
tioned, but also hath renewed, or caused to be renewed, the said war
against the Parliament and good people of this nation in this present year
1648, in the Counties of Kent, Essex, Surrey, Sussex, Middlesex, and
many other Counties and places in England and Wales, and also by sea.
And particularly he, the said Charles Stuart, hath for that purpose given
commission to his son the Prince, and others, whereby, besides multitudes
of other persons, many such as were by the Parliament entrusted and employed for the safety of the nation (being by him or his agents corrupted to
the betraying of their trust, and revolting from the Parliament), have had
entertainment and commission for the continuing and renewing of war and
hostility against the said Parliament and people as aforesaid. By which
cruel and unnatural wars, by him, the said Charles Stuart, levied, continued, and renewed as aforesaid, much innocent blood of the free people
of this nation hath been spilt, many families have been undone, the public
treasure wasted and exhausted, trade obstructed and miserably decayed,
vast expense and damage to the nation incurred, and many parts of this
land spoiled, some of them even to desolation. And for further prosecution of his said evil designs, he, the said Charles Stuart, doth still continue his commissions to the said Prince, and other rebels and revolters,
both English and foreigners, and to the Earl of Ormond, and the Irish rebels and revolters associated with him; from whom further invasions upon
this land are threatened, upon the procurement, and on the behalf of the
said Charles Stuart.

All which wicked designs, wars, and evil practices of him, the said
Charles Stuart, have been, and are carried on for the advancement and up-
holding of a personal interest of will, power, and pretended prerogative
to himself and his family, against the public interest, common right, liberty, justice, and peace of the people of this nation, by and from whom he
was entrusted as aforesaid.

By all which it appeareth that the said Charles Stuart hath been, and
is the occasioner, author, and continuer of the said unnatural, cruel and
bloody wars; and therein guilty of all the treasons, murders, rapines,

burnings, spoils, desolations, damages and mischiefs to this nation, acted
and committed in the said wars, or occasioned thereby.

THE INSTRUMENT OF GOVERNMENT, December 16, 1653

Source: Guy C. Lee, ed., Source-Book of English History. Leading Documents...(New York: H. Holt and Company, 1900) pp. 377-387.

> The Puritan Revolution produced many im-
> portant ideas on government which were to
> help shape the future constitutional develop -
> ment of Great Britain. The form of Govern-
> ment created under the leadership of Oliver
> Cromwell illustrates the important advances
> which had been made in the constitutional
> theory. The forms of government are care-
> fully developed in this document.

The government of the Commonwealth of England, Scotland, and Ireland, and the dominions thereunto belonging.

I. That the supreme legislative authority of the Commonwealth of
England, Scotland, and Ireland, and the dominions thereunto belonging,
shall be and reside in one person, and the people assembled in Parliament:
the style of which person shall be the Lord Protector of the Commonwealth
of England, Scotland, and Ireland.

II. That the exercise of the chief magistracy and the administration
of the government over the said countries and dominions, and the people
thereof, shall be in the Lord Protector, assisted with a council, the number where of shall not exceed twenty-one, nor be less than thirteen .

III. That all writs, processes, commissions, patents, grants, and
other things, which no run in the name and style of the keepers of the liberty of England by authority of Parliament, shall run in the name and style
of the Lord Protector, from whom, for the future, shall be derived all
magistracy and honours in these three nations; and have the power of par-
dons (except in case of murders and treason) and benefit of all forfeitures
for the public use; and shall govern the said countries and dominions in
all things by the advice of the council, and according to these presents and
the laws.

IV. That the Lord Protector, the Parliament sitting, shall dispose and
order the militia and forces, both by sea and land, for the peace and good
of the three nations, by consent of Parliament; and that the Lord Protector,
with the advice and consent of the major part of the council, shall dispose
and order the militia for the ends aforesaid in the intervals of Parliament.

V. That the Lord Protector, by the advice aforesaid, shall direct in
all things concerning the keeping and holding of a good correspondency
with foreign kings, princes, and states; and also, with the consent of the
major part of the council, have the power of war and peace.

VI. That the laws shall not be altered, suspended, abrogated, or repealed, nor any new law made, nor any tax, charge, or imposition laid upon the people, but by common consent in Parliament, save only as is expressed in the thirtieth article.

VII. That there shall be a Parliament summoned to meet at Westminster upon the third day of September, 1654, and that successively a Parliament shall be summoned once in every third year, to be accounted from
the dissolution of the present Parliament.

VIII. That neither the Parliament to be next summoned, nor any successive Parliaments, shall, during the time of five months, to be accounted
from the day of their first meeting, be adjourned, prorogued, or dissolved,
without their own consent.

****

XXIII. That the Lord Protector, with the advice of the major part of
the Council, shall at any other time than is before expressed, when the necessities of the State shall require it, summon Parliaments in manner before expressed, which shall not be adjourned, prorogued, or dissolved
without their own consent, during the first three months of their sitting.
And in case of future war with any foreign State a Parliament shall be forthwith summoned for their advice concerning the same.

XXIV. That all Bills agreed unto by the Parliament, shall be presented
to the Lord Protector for his consent; and in case he shall not give his consent thereto within twenty days after they shall be presented to him, or
give satisfaction to the Parliament within the time limited, that then, upon
declaration of the Parliament that the Lord Protector hath not consented
nor given satisfaction, such Bills shall pass into and become laws, although
he shall not give his consent thereunto; provided such Bills contain nothing
in them contrary to the matters contained in these presents.

****

XXX. That the raising of money for defraying the charge of the present extraordinary forces, both at sea and land, in respect of the present
wars, shall be by consent of Parliament, and not otherwise; save only that
the Lord Protector, with the consent of the major part of the Council, for
preventing the disorders and dangers which might otherwise fall out both
by sea and land, shall have power, until the meeting of the first Parliament,
to raise money for the purposes aforesaid; and also to make laws and ordinances for the peace and welfare of these nations where it shall be necessary, which shall be binding and in force, until order shall be taken in
Parliament concerning the same.

XXXI. That the lands, tenements, rents, royalties, jurisdictions and
hereditaments which remain yet unsold or undisposed of, by Act or Ordinance of Parliament, belonging to the Commonwealth (except the forests
and chases, and the honours and manors belonging to the same; the lands
of the rebels in Ireland, lying in the four counties of Dublin, Cork, Kil-
dare, and Carlow; the lands forfeited by the people of Scotland in the late

wars, and also the lands of Papists and delinquents in England who have not
yet compounded), shall be vested in the Lord Protector, to hold, to him
and his successors, Lords Protectors of these nations, and shall not be
alienated but by consent in Parliament. And all debts, fines, issues,
amercements, penalties and profits, certain and casual, due to the Keepers of the liberties of England by authority of Parliament, shall be due to
the Lord Protector, and be payable into his public receipt, and shall be re-
covered and prosecuted in his name.

XXX. That the office of Lord Protector over these nations shall be
elective and not hereditary; and upon the death of the Lord Protector, another fit person shall be forthwith elected to succeed him in the Government; which election shall be by the Council, who, immediately upon the
death of the Lord Protector, shall assemble in the Chamber where they
usually sit in Council; and, having given notice to all their members of the
cause of their assembling, shall being thirteen at least present, proceed
to the election; and, before they depart the said Chamber, shall elect a
fit person to succeed in the Government, and forthwith cause proclamation
thereof to be made in all the three nations as shall be requisite; and the
person that they, or the major part of them, shall elect as aforesaid, shall
be, and shall be taken to be, Lord Protector over these nations of England,
Scotland and Ireland, and the dominions thereto belonging. Provided that
none of the children of the late King, nor any of his line or family, be
elected to be Lord Protector or other Chief Magistrate over these nations,
or any the dominions thereto belonging. And until the aforesaid election
be past, the Council shall take care of the Government, and administer in
all things as full as the Lord Protector, or the Lord Protector and Council
are enabled to do.

XXXIII. That Oliver Cromwell, Captain-General of the forces of England, Scotland and Ireland, shall be, and is hereby declared to be, Lord
Protector of the Commonwealth of England, Scotland and Ireland, and the
dominions thereto belonging, for his life.

XXXIV. That the Chancellor, Keeper or Commissioners of the Great
Seal, the Treasurer, Admiral, Chief Governors of Ireland and Scotland,
and the Chief Justices of both the Benches, shall be chosen by the approbation of Parliament; and, in the intervals of Parliament, by the approbation
of the major part of the Council, to be afterwards approved by the Parliament.

XXXV. That the Christian religion, as contained in the Scriptures, be
held forth and recommended as the public profession of these nations; and
that, as soon as may be, a provision, less subject to scruple and contention, and more certain than the present, be made for the encouragement
and maintenance of able and painful teachers, for the instructing the people,
and for discovery and confutation of error, hereby, and whatever is contrary to sound doctrine; and until such provision be made, the present maintenance shall not be taken away or impeached. . . .

THE BILL OF RIGHTS, FEBRUARY 12, 1689

Source: Guy C. Lee, ed. Source-Book of English History. Leading Documents... (New York: H. Holt and Company, 1900) pp 424-431.

The Stuart Monarchy had been restored in
1660, and the nation had endured many differences with Charles II, who ruled until 1685,
and his borther James II, who ruled from
1685 to 1688. The latter had publicly proclaimed
himself a Catholic during his brother's reign,
and Parliament attempted to exclude him from
the succession several times. When James
came to the throne he proceeded to disallow
laws which prohibited Catholics from holding
office. When James' wife gave birth to a son
which was a guarantee of the perpetuation of a
Catholic monarchy, the Tories decided to join
with the Whigs in opposition to the King. They
invited James' daughter Mary and her husband
William, Prince of Orange, to come to England
and eventually become joint sovereigns. Among
the legislation which the Parliament passed during the Glorious Revolution, the Bill of Rights
stands as one of the most important expressions
of the basic rights of all Englishmen.

BILL OF RIGHTS

Whereas the Lords Spiritual and Temporal, and Commons, assembled
at Westminster, lawfully, fully, and freely representing all the estates of
the people of this realm, did, upon the thirteenth day of February, in the
year of our Lord one thousand six hundred eight-eight, present unto their
Majesties, then called and known by the names and style of William and
Mary, Prince and Princess of Orange, being present in their proper persons, a certain declaration in writing, made by the said Lords and Commons, in the words following; viz: --
Whereas the late King James II., by the assistance of diverse evil
counsellors, judges, and ministers employed by him, did endeavour to
subvert and extirpate the Protestant religion, and the laws and liberties
of this kingdom: --
1. By assuming and exercising a power of dispensing with and suspending of laws, and the execution of laws, without consent of Parliament.
2. By committing and prosecuting divers worthy prelates, for humbly

petitioning to be excused from concurring to the same assumed power.

3. By issuing and causing to be executed a commission under the Great Seal for erecting a court, called the Court of Commissioners for Ecclesiastical Causes.

4. By levying money for and to the use of the Crown, by pretence of prerogative, for other time, and in other manner than the same was granted by Parliament.

5. By raising and keeping a standing army within this kingdom in time of peace, without consent of Parliament, and quartering soldiers contrary to law.

6. By causing several good subjects, being Protestants, to be disarmed, at the same time when Papists were both armed and employed contrary to law.

7. By violating the freedom of election of members to serve in Parliament.

8. By prosecutions in the Court of King's Bench, for matters and causes cognizable only in Parliament: and by diverse other arbitrary and illegal courses.

9. And whereas of late years, partial, corrupt, and unqualified persons have been returned and served on juries in trials, and particularly diverse jurors in trials for high treason, which were not freeholders.

10. And excessive bail hath been required of persons committed in criminal cases, to elude the benefit of the laws made for the liberty of the subjects.

11. And excessive fines have been imposed; and illegal and cruel punishments inflicted.

12. And several grants and promises made of fines and forfeitures, before any conviction or judgment against the persons upon whom the same were to be levied.

All which are utterly and directly contrary to the known laws and statutes, and freedom of this realm.

And whereas the said late King James II, having abdicated the government, and the throne being thereby vacant, his Highness the Prince of Orange (whom it hath pleased Almighty God to make the glorious instrument of delivering this kingdom from popery and arbitrary power) did (by the advice of the Lords Spiritual and Temporal, and diverse principal persons of the Commons) cause letters to be written to the Lords Spiritual and Temporal, being Protestants, and other letters to the several counties, cities, universities, boroughs, and cinque ports, for the choosing of such persons as represent them, as were of right to be sent to Parliament, to meet and sit at Westminster upon the two-and twentieth day of January, in this year one thousand six hundred eighty and eight, in order to such an establishment, as that their religion, laws and liberties might not again be in danger of being subverted; upon which letters, elections have been accordingly made.

And thereupon the said Lords Spiritual and Temporal, and Commons,

pursuant to their respective letters and elections, being now assembled
in a full and free representation of this nation, taking into their most serious consideration the best means for attaining the ends aforesaid, do in the
first place (as their ancestors in like case have usually done), for the vin-
dicating and asserting their ancient rights and liberties, declare: --

1. That the pretended power of suspending of laws, or the execution
of laws, by regal authority, without consent of parliament, is illegal.

2. That the pretended power of dispensing with laws, or the execution
of laws by regal authority, as it hath been assumed and exercised of late,
is illegal.

3. That the commission for erecting the late Court of Commissioners
for Ecclesiastical causes, and all other commissions and courts of like
nature, are illegal and pernicious.

4. That levying money for or to the use of the Crown, by pretence of
prerogative, without grant of parliament, for longer time or in other manner than the same is or shall be granted, is illegal.

5. That it is the right of the subjects to petition the king, and all com-
mitments and prosecutions for such petitioning are illegal.

6. That the raising or keeping a standing army within the kingdom in
time of peace, unless it be with consent of parliament, is against law.

7. That the subjects which are Protestants may have arms for their
defence suitable to their conditions, and as allowed by law.

8. That election of members of parliament ought to be free.

9. That the freedom of speech, and debates or proceedings in parliament, ought not to be impeached or questioned in any court or place out of
parliament.

10. That excessive bail ought not to be required, nor excessive fines
imposed; nor cruel and unusual punishments inflicted.

11. That jurors ought to be duly impanelled and returned and jurors
which pass upon men in trials for high treason ought to be freeholders.

12. That all grants and promises of fines and forfeitures of particular persons before conviction, are illegal and void.

13. And that for redress of all grievances and for the amending,
strengthening, and preserving of the laws, parliament ought to be held
frequently.

*****

NORTH BRITON NO. 45, April 23, 1763

Source: Guy C. Lee, ed. Source-Book of English History. Leading Documents... (New York: H. Holt and Company, 1900) pp. 467-473.

John Wilkes, who had always been an incisive critic of the government, made specific comments upon the King's speech when Parliament was prorogued and upon the peace which had recently been concluded. It was denounced by the Royal Court as libel and insulting to the King. Wilke's believed that the King's speech was that of the Ministry. Wilkes was tried for libel and convicted. He was imprisoned, but was reelected to Parliament after he had been removed from office by that body. After several elections each of which Wilkes won, the Commons finally declared his opponent duly elected. The following selection taken from the North Briton illustrates the attacks made by Wilkes.

THE NORTH BRITON
No. XLV, Saturday, April 23, 1763

Genus orationis atrox, et vehemens, cui opponitur lenitatis et mansuetudinis.
CICERO.

The King's Speech has always been considered by the legislature, and by the public at large, as the Speech of the Minister. It has regularly, at the beginning of every session of parliament, been referred by both houses to the consideration of a committee, and has been generally canvassed with the utmost freedom, when the minister of the crown has been obnoxious to the nation. The ministers of this free country, conscious of the undoubted privileges of so spirited a people, and with the terrors of parliament before their eyes, have ever been cautious, no less with regard to the matter, than to the expressions, of speeches, which they have advised the sovereign to make from the throne, at the opening of every session. They well knew that an honest house of parliament, true to their trust, could not fail to detect the fallacious arts, or to remonstrate against the daring acts of violence, committed by any minister. The speech at the close of the session has ever been considered as the most secure method of promulgating the favourite court creed among the vulgar; because the parliament, which is the constitutional guardian of the liberties of the people, has in this case no opportunity of remonstrating, or of impeaching any wicked servant of the crown.

This week has given the public the most abandoned instance of ministerial effrontery ever attempted to be imposed on mankind. The minister's speech of last Tuesday, is not to be paralleled in the annals of this country. I am in doubt, whether the imposition is greater on the sovereign, or on the nation. Every friend of his country must lament that a prince of so many great and amiable qualities, whom England truly reveres, can be brought to give the sanction of his sacred name to the most odious measures, and to the most unjustifiable, public declarations, from a throne ever renowned for truth, honour, and unsullied virtue. I am sure, all foreigners, especially the king of Prussia, will hold the minister in contempt and abhorrence. He has made our sovereign declare, My expectations have been fully answered by the happy effects which the several allies of my crown have derived from this salutary measure of the definitive Treaty. The powers at war with my good brother, the King of Prussia, have been induced to agree to such terms of accomodation, as that great prince has approved; and the success which has attended my negociation, has necessarily and immediately diffused the blessings of peace through every part of Europe. The infamous fallacy of this whole sentence is apparent to all mankind: for it is known, that the King of Prussia did not barely approve, but absolutely dictated, as conqueror, every article of the terms of peace. No advantage of any kind has accrued to that magnanimous prince from our negociations, but he was basely deserted by the Scottish prime-minister of England. He was known by every court in Europe to be scarcely on better terms of friendship here, than at Vienna; and he was betrayed by us in the treaty of peace. What a strain of insolence, therefore, is it in a minister to lay claim to what he is conscious all his efforts tended to prevent, and meanly to arrogate to himself a share in the fame and glory of one of the greatest princes the world has ever seen? The king of Prussia, however, has gloriously kept all his former conquests, and stipulated security for all his allies, even for the elector of Hanover. I know in what light this great prince is considered in Europe, and in what manner he has been treated here; among other reasons, perhaps, from some contemptuous expressions he may have used of the Scot: expressions which are every day echoed by the whole body of Englishmen through the southern part of this island.

The Preliminary Articles of Peace were such as have drawn the contempt of mankind on our wretched negociators. All our most valuable conquests were agreed to be restored, and the East India Company would have been infallibly ruined by a single article of this fallacious and baneful negociation. No hireling of the minister has been hardy enough to dispute this; yet the minister himself has made our sovereign declare, the satisfaction which he felt at the approaching re-establishment of peace upon conditions so honourable to his crown, and so beneficial to his people. As to the entire approbation of parliament, which is so vainly boasted of, the world knows how that was obtained. The large debt on the <u>Civil List,</u> already above half a year in arrear, shews pretty clearly the transactions of the winter. It is, however, remarkable, that the minister's speeche dwells on the <u>entire approbation</u> given by parliament to the <u>Preliminary Articles,</u> which I will venture to say, he must by this time be ashamed of; for he has been brought to confess the total want of that knowledge, accuracy and precision, by which such immense advantages both of trade and territory, were sacrificed to our inveterate enemies. These gross blunders are, indeed, in some measure set right by the <u>Definitive Treaty:</u> yet, the most important articles, relative to <u>cessions,</u> <u>commerce,</u> and the FISHERY, remain as they were; with respect to the French. . . .

PROCLAMATION PREVENTING SEDITIOUS MEETINGS
AND WRITINGS, May 21, 1792

Source: The Annual Register, 1792. (London, 1793) pp. 158-160.

> The French Revolution had created such a fever-
> ish state of excitement in Europe that the clamor
> for reform was great. As relations between Eng-
> land and France began to deteriorate, and as re-
> formers became agitated the government decided
> to prevent serious disturbances by banning any
> seditious writings and meetings in the following
> proclamation.

His Majesty's Proclamation for prevention Seditious Meetings
and Writings, May 21, 1792

By the King --   A PROCLAMATION.

George Rex.

Whereas divers wicked and seditious writings have been printed, published, and industriously dispersed, tending to excite tumult and disorder,
by endeavoring to raise groundless jealousies and discontents in the minds
of our faithful and loving subjects respecting the laws and happy constitution of government, civil and religious, established in this kingdom, and
endeavouring to vilify and bring into contempt the wise and wholesome provisions made at the time of the glorious Revolution, and since strengthened
and confirmed by subsequent laws, for the preservation and security of the
rights and liberties of our faithful and loving subjects: and whereas divers
writings have also been printed, published, and industriously dispersed,
recommending the said wicked and seditious publications to the attention of
all our faithful and loving subjects: and whereas we have also reason to believe, that correspondences have been entered into with sundry persons
in foreign parts, with a view to forward the criminal and wicked purposes
above mentioned: and whereas the wealth, happiness, and prosperity of this
kingdom do, under Divine Providence, chiefly depend upon a due submission to the laws, a just confidence in the integrity and wisdom of parliament, and a continuance of that zealous attachment to the government and
constitution of the kingdom, which has ever prevailed in the minds of the
people thereof: and whereas there is nothing which we so earnestly desire
as to secure the public peace and prosperity, and to preserve to all our
loving subjects the full enjoyment of their rights and liberties, both religious and civil; we therefore being resolved, as far as in us lies, to repress

the wicked and seditious practices aforesaid, and to deter all persons from following so pernicious an example, have thought fit, by the advice of our privy council, to issue this our royal proclamation, solemnly warning all our loving subjects, as they tender their own happiness and that of their posterity, to guard against all such attempts which aim at the subversion of all regular government within this kingdom, and which are inconsistent with the peace and order of society; and earnestly exhorting them, at all times, and to the utmost of their power, to avoid and discourage all proceedings tending to produce riots and tumults. And we do strictly charge and command all our magistrates in and throughout our kingdom of Great Britain, that they do make diligent inquiry, in order to discover the authors and printers of such wicked and seditious writings as aforesaid, and all others who shall disperse the same; and we do further charge and command all our sheriffs, justices of the peace, chief magistrates of our cities, boroughs, and corporations, and all other our officers and magistrates throughout our kingdom of Great Britain, that they do, in their several and respective stations, take the most immediate and effectual care to suppress and prevent all riots, tumults, and other disorders, which may be attempted to be raised or made by any person or persons; which, on whatever pretext they may be grounded, are not only contrary to law, but dangerous to the most important interests of this kingdom: and we do further require and command all and every our magistrates aforesaid, that they do, from time to time, transmit to one of our principal secretaries of state due and full information of such persons as shall be found offending as aforesaid, or in any degree aiding or abetting therein; it being our determination, for the preservation of the peace and happiness of our faithful and loving subjects, to carry the laws vigorously into execution against such offenders as aforesaid.

Given at our court at the Queen's House, the 21st
day of May, 1792, in the 32d year of our reign.

GOD SAVE THE KING.

THE REGENCY ACT, February 4, 1811

Source: Hansard's Parliamentary Debates, 1st Series, Vol. XVIII, 1810-1811, pp. 1126-1144.

> King George III had become insane in 1788, and
> a Regency Bill had been passed at that time. But
> before George, Prince of Wales, could take over
> as Regent his father regained his senses. When
> the King became ill again in 1811 the Parliament
> passed a second Regency Act, sections of which
> are printed below. The Tories who were in office
> at the time inserted a provision that the Regent
> could not change any Ministers until one year had
> passed in order to prevent him from immediately
> appointing his Whig friends to office. When the
> year passed Prince George found that he had Tory
> sympathies and continued to support his ministers.

An Act to Provide for the Administration of the Royal Authority and for the Care of His Majesty's Royal Person, During the Continuance of His Majesty's Illness; and for the Resumption of the Exercise of the Royal Authority by His Majesty

Whereas by reason of the sheer Indisposition with which it has pleased God to afflict the King's most excellent Majesty the personal exercise of the Royal Authority by His Majesty is for the present so far interrupted that it becomes necessary to make provisions for assisting His Majesty in the administration and exercise of the Royal Authority, and also for the care of His Royal Person during the continuance of His Majesty's Indisposition, and for the Resumption of the exercise of the Royal Authority by His Majesty; Be it therefore enacted by the King's most excellent Majesty, by and with the advice and consent of the Lords Spiritual and Temporal and Commons, in this present Parliament assembled, and by the authority of the same, That His Royal Highness George Augustus Frederick Prince of Wales shall have full Power and Authority in the name and on the behalf of His Majesty, and under the Style and Title of "Regent of the United Kingdom of Great Britain and Ireland, " to exercise and administer the Royal Power and Authority to the Crown of the United Kingdom of Great Britain and Ireland belonging, and to use, execute, and perform all authorities, prerogatives, acts of Government and administration of the same, which lawfully belong to the King of the said United Kingdom to use, execute, and perform; subject to such Limitations, Exceptions, Regulations, and Re-

strictions, as are herein-after specified and contained; and all and every
Act and Acts which shall be done by the said Regent, in the name and on
behalf of His Majesty, by virtue and in pursuance of this Act, and according to the powers and authorities hereby vested in him, shall have the same
force and effect to all intents and purposes as the like Acts would have if
done by His Majesty himself, and shall to all intents and purposes be full
and sufficient warrant to all persons acting under the authority thereof;
and all persons shall yield obedience thereto, and carry the same into effect, in the same manner and for the same purposes as the same persons
ought to yield obedience to and carry into effect the like acts done by His
Majesty himself; and any law, course of office, or other matter or thing
to the contrary notwithstanding.

II.   And be it further enacted, That as to all authorities given and appointments made in the name and in the behalf of His Majesty, and all other
acts, matters, and things usually done under the authority of Royal Sign
Manual, the Signature of the Regent in the form following, that is to say,
"George P. R. " or in cases where the Royal Signature has usually be affixed
in initials only, then in the form "G. P. R. , " shall be as valid and effectual,
and have the same force and effect as His Majesty's Royal Sign Manual,
and shall be deemed and taken to be to all intents and purposes His Majesty's Royal Sign Manual, and be obeyed as much.

III.   And be it further enacted, That when His Majesty shall by the
blessing of God be restored to such a state of health as to be capable of resuming the personal exercise of His Royal Authority, and shall have declared His Royal Will and Pleasure thereupon, as herein-after provided,
all and every power and authority, given by this Act, for the exercise and
administration of His Royal Power and Authority, or for the using, execut-
ing, and performing the Authorities, Prerogatives, Acts of Government,
and Administration of the same, which belong to the King of the United
Kingdom of Great Britain and Ireland to use, execute, and perform, or for
the care His Majesty's Royal Person, shall cease and determine; and no
act, matter, or thing, which, under this Act, and previous to such declaration might be done in the administration of His Majesty's Royal Power
and Authority, or in the using, exercising, or performing any such Authorities, Prerogatives, Acts of Government, or Administration, as aforesaid,
or in the care of His Majesty's Royal Person, by virtue and in pursuance
of this Act, shall, if done after such declaration of His Majesty's Royal
Will and Pleasure, be thenceforth valid or effectual.

IV.   Provided always, and be it further enacted, That all persons holding Offices or Places or Pensions, during His Majesty's Pleasure, at the
time of such declaration, under any appointment or authority of the Regent,
or Her Majesty, under the provisions of this Act, shall continue to hold
the same, and to use, exercise, and enjoy all the powers, authorities, privileges, and emoluments thereof, notwithstanding such declarations of the
resumption of the Royal Authority by His Majesty, unless and until His
Majesty shall declare His Royal Will and Pleasure to the contrary; and all

Orders, Acts of Government, or Administration of His Majesty's Royal
Authority, ..., issued, or done by the said Regent, before such declaration, shall be and remain in full force and effect, until the same shall be
countermanded by His Majesty.

V. Provided also, and be it further enacted, That no Acts of Legal
Power; Prerogative, Government, or Administration of Government, of
what kind or nature soever, which might lawfully be done or executed by
the King's most excellent Majesty, personally exercising His Royal Authority, shall, during the continuance of the Regency by this Act established,
be valid and effectual, unless done and executed in the name and on the behalf of His Majesty, by the Authority of the said Regent, according to the
provisions of this Act, and subject to the Limitations, Exceptions, Regulations, and Restrictions hereinafter contained.

XI. And be it enacted, That nothing in this Act contained shall extend
or be construed to extend to impower the said Regent, in the name and on
behalf of His Majesty, to give the Royal Assent to any Bill or Bills in Parliament for repealing, changing or in any respect varying the Order and
Course of Succession to the Crown of this Realm, as the same stands now
established by an Act passed in the twelfth year of the reign of William the
third, ...

XIX. And whereas it is necessary that effectual provision should be
made that His Majesty may resume the personal exercise of His Royal Authority, as soon as His Majesty is restored to such a state of health as to
be capable of resuming the same; Be it therefore enacted, That when it
shall appear to Her Majesty the Queen, and to any four or more of the Council appointed by this Act to assist Her Majesty in the execution of the trust
committed to Her Majesty by this Act, assembled at any meeting held in
pursuance of Her Majesty's Royal Will and Pleasure signified for that purpose, or assembled under the direction of this Act, or in pursuance of His
Majesty's Royal Will and Pleasure signified to Her Majesty and Her Council for that purpose, which presence of Her Majesty, upon His Majesty's
Royal Will and Pleasure being signified for that purpose, that His Majesty
is restored to such a state of Health as to be capable of resuming the personal Exercise of the Royal Authority it shall and may be lawful for Her
said Majesty, by the advice of any four or more of Her said Council, to no-
tify the same by an Instrument under Majesty's Hand and signed also by the
said four or more of Her Majesty's Council, and addressed to the Lord
President of His Majesty's most Hon. Privy Council for the time being, or
in his absence to one of His Majesty's Principal Secretaries of State; and
said Lord President or Secretary of State shall and is hereby required, under the seat thereof to communicate the same to the said Regent, and to
summon forthwith a Privy Council, and the members of His Majesty's most
Hon. Privy Council are hereby required to assemble in consequence of such
Summons; and the said Lord President, or in his absence the said Secretary
of State, is required, to cause said Instrument to be entered on the Books
of the said Privy Council....

THE PARLIAMENTARY REFORM BILL, June 7, 1832

Source: Hansard's Parliamentary Debates, 3rd Series, Vol. XIII, 1832,
Appendix, pp. 33-68.

> Parliamentary Reform had been an issue for many
> years. The French Revolutionary and Napoleonic
> Wars had caused a reaction in England which vir-
> tually put a stop to any reforms for 40 years.
> During the early 1830's the cry for a change in the
> old system of Parliamentary representation could
> no longer be ignored. The Act which was passed
> eliminated certain rotten boroughs, reduced the
> representation of others, as well as created new
> ones. In addition qualifications for suffrage were
> lowered so that many members of the Middle Class
> were given the vote.

An Act to Amend the Representation of the People
in England and Wales.

Preamble. Whereas it is expedient to take effectual Measures for
"correcting divers Abuses that have long prevailed in the Choice of Members to serve in the Commons House of Parliament, to deprive many incon-
siderable Places of the Right of returning Members, to grant such privileges to large, populous, and wealthy Towns, to increase the Number of
Knights of the Shire to extend Elective Franchise to many of His Majesty's
Subjects who have not heretofore enjoyed the same, and to diminish the Ex-
pence of Elections:" and be it therefore enacted by the KING's Most Excellent Majesty, by and with the Advice and Consent of the Lords Spiritual
and Temporal, and Commons in this present Parliament assembled, and
by the authority of the same, ...

> (Follows ending of Rotten Boroughs, Limiting of Bor-
> oughs to one member, creates new boroughs, lists of voters,
> and other pertinent information.)

VII. (Boundaries of existing Boroughs in England to be settled.) And
be it enacted, That every City and Borough in England which now returns
a member or Members to serve in Parliament, and every Place sharing in
the Election therewith, ... shall, ..., include the Place or Places respectively which shall be settled and described by an Act to be passed for that
Purpose in this present Parliament, which Act, when passed, shall be
deemed and taken to be part of this Act as fully and effectually as if the
same were incorporated herewith ....

LXXVII. (This Act not to extend to Universities of Oxford and Cambridge.)

And provided always, and be it enacted, That nothing in this Act contained shall extend to or in any wise affect the Election of Members to serve in Parliament for the Universities of <u>Oxford</u> or <u>Cambridge</u>, or shall entitle any person to vote in the Elections of members to serve in Parliament for the City of <u>Oxford</u> or Town of <u>Cambridge</u> in respect of the Occupation of any Chambers or Premises in any of the Colleges or Halls of the Universities of <u>Oxford</u> or <u>Cambridge</u>.

LXXIX. And be it enacted, That throughout this act wherever the Words "City or Borough" "Cities or Boroughs" may occur, those Words shall be construed to include, except there be something in the Subject or Context manifestly repugnant to such Construction, all Towns Corporate, Cinque Ports, Districts, or Places within <u>England</u> and <u>Wales</u> which shall be entitled after this Act shall have passed to return a Member or Members to serve in Parliament, other than Counties at large, and Ridings, Parts and Visions of Counties at large, ...

CHARTISM: THE FIRST NATIONAL PETITION, 1838

Source: Guy C. Lee, ed. Source-Book of English History. Leading Documents...(New York: H. Holt and Company, 1900) pp. 530-533.

> The lower classes had been dissatisfied with the
> limited changes provided by the Reform Act of
> 1832. In the first Charter the petitioner indi-
> cated their concern with problems evident in
> England and made six proposals for Parliamen-
> tary Reform: universal suffrage, the secret
> ballot, annual parliaments, removal of property
> qualifications for membership in Parliament,
> equal electoral districts, and payment of mem-
> bers of Parliament. Three Petitions were pre-
> sented, each of which was rejected -- the last
> in 1848.

"To the Honourable the Commons of Great Britain and Ireland, in Parliament assembled, the Petition of the undersigned, their suffering countrymen,

"HUMBLY SHOWETH, --

"That we, your petitioners, dwell in a land whose merchants are noted for their enterprise, whose manufacturers are very skilful, and whose workmen are proverbial for their industry. The land itself is goodly, the soil rich, and the temperature wholesome. It is abundantly furnished with the materials of commerce and trade. It has numerous and convenient harbours. In facility of internal communication it exceeds all others. For three and twenty years we have enjoyed a profound peace. Yet, with all the elements of national prosperity, and with every disposition and capacity to take advantage of them, we find ourselves with public and private suffering. We are bowed down under a load of taxes, which, notwithstanding, fall greatly short of the wants of our rulers. Our traders are trembling on the verge of bankruptcy; our workmen are starving. Capital brings no profit, and labour no remuneration. The home of the artificer is desolate, and the warehouse of the pawnbroker is full. The workhouse is crowded, and the manufactory is deserted. We have looked on every side; we have searched diligently in order to find out the causes of distress so sore and so long continued. We can discover none in nature or in Providence. Heaven has dealt graciously by the people, nor have the people abused its grace, but the foolishness of our rulers has made the goodness of our God of none effect. The energies of a mighty kingdom have been

wasted in building up the power of selfish and ignorant men, and its re-
sources squandered for their aggrandisement. The good of a part has been
advanced at the sacrifice of the good of the nation. The few have governed
for the interest of the few, while the interests of the many have been sot-
tishly neglected, or insolently and tyrannously trampled upon. It was the
fond expectation of the friends of the people that a remedy for the greater
part, if not for the whole of their grievances, would be found in the Reform
Act of 1832. They regarded that Act as a wise means to a worthy end, as
the machinery of an improved legislation, where the will of the masses
would be at length potential. They have been bitterly and basely deceived.
The fruit which looked so fair to the eye, has turned to dust and ashes when
gathered. The Reform Act effected a transfer of power from one domineer-
ing faction to another, and left the people as helpless as before. Our slavery has been exchanged for an apprenticeship of liberty, which has aggra-
vated the painful feelings of our social degradation, by adding to them the
sickening of still deferred hope. We come before your honourable house to
tell you, with all humility, that this state of things must not be permitted to
continue. That it cannot long continue, without very seriously endangering
the stability of the throne, and the peace of the kingdom, and that if, by
God's help, and all lawful and constitutional appliances, and end can be put
to it, we are fully resolved that it shall speedily come to an end. We tell
your honourable house, that the capital of the master must no longer be deprived of its due profit; that the labour of the workman must no longer be
deprived of its due reward. That the laws which make food dear, and the
laws which make money scarce, must be abolished. That taxation must be
made to all on property, not on industry. That the good of the many, as it
is the only legitimate end, so must it be the sole study of the government.
As a preliminary essential to these and other requisite changes -- as the
means by which alone the interests of the people can be effectually vindicated and secured, we demand that those interests be confided to the keeping
of the people. When the State calls for defenders, when it calls for money,
no consideration of poverty or ignorance can be pleaded in refusal or delay
of the call. Required, as we are universally, to support and obey the laws,
nature and reason entitle us to demand that in the making of the laws the
universal voice shall be implicitly listened to. We perform the duties of
freemen; we must have the privileges of freemen. Therefore, we demand
universal suffrage. The suffrage, to be exempt from the corruption of the
wealthy and the violence of the powerful, must be secret. The assertion
of our right necessarily involves the power of our uncontrolled exercise.
We ask for the reality of a good, not for its semblance, therefore we demand the ballot. The connection between the Representatives and the
people, to be beneficial, must be intimate. The legislative and constituent
powers, for correction and for instruction, ought to be brought into frequent contact. Errors which are comparatively light, when susceptible of
a speedy popular remedy, may produce the most disastrous effects when
permitted to grow inveterate through years of compulsory endurance. To

public safety, as well as public confidence, frequent elections are essential. Therefore, we demand annual parliaments. With power to choose, and freedom in choosing, the range of our choice must be unrestricted. We are compelled, by the existing laws, to take for our representatives men who are incapable of appreciating our difficulties, or have little sympathy with them; merchants who have retired from trade and no longer feel its harrassings; proprietors of land who are alike ignorant of its evils and its cure; lawyers by whom the notoriety of the senate is courted only as a means of obtaining notice in the courts. The labours of a representative who is sedulous in the discharge of his duty are numerous and burdensome. It is neither just nor reasonable, nor safe, that they should continue to be gratuitously rendered. We demand that in the future election of members of your honourable house, the approbation of the constituency shall be the sole qualification, and that to every representative so chosen, shall be assigned out of the public taxes, a fair and adequate remuneration for the time which he is called upon to devote to the pubic service. The management of this mighty kingdom is hitherto been a subject for contending factions to try their selfish experiments upon. We have felt the consequences in our sorrowful experience. Short glimmerings of uncertain enjoyment, swallowed up by long and dark seasons of suffering. If the self-government of the people should not remove their distresses, it will, at least, remove their repinings. Universal suffrage will, and it only can, bring true and lasting peace to the nation; we firmly believe that it will also bring prosperity. May it therefore please your honourable house, to take this our petition into your most serious consideration, and to use your utmost endeavours, by all constitutional means, to have a law passed, granting to every male of lawful age, sane mind, and unconvicted of crime, the right of voting for members of parliament to be in the way of secret ballot, and ordaining that the duration of parliament, so chose, shall in no case exceed one year, and abolishing all property qualifications in the members, and providing for their due remuneration while in attendance on their parliamentary duties.

"And your petitioners shall ever pray."

JEWISH EMANCIPATION, July 23, 1858

Source: The Annual Register, 1858. (London: Longman & Co., 1859)

The British Parliament had been slowly emancipating various religious groups. The Dissenters were first granted the right to serve in Parliament, followed by the Catholics. The latter were granted emancipation in 1829 as a result of the election of the popular Daniel O'Connel in Ireland. Finally, the government recognized the injustices which prevailed in the disabilities placed upon the Jews. This act placed them on an equal footing with other groups and granted them admission to Parliament.

1858 CHAPTER 49

An Act to Provide for the Relief of Her Majesty's Subjects Professing the Jewish Religion

Be it enacted by the Queen's Most Excellent Majesty, by and with the Advice and Consent and Lords Spiritual and Temporal, and Commons, in this present Parliament assembled, and by the Authority of the same, as follows:

I. Where it shall appear to either House of Parliament that a Person professing the Jewish Religion, otherwise entitled to sit and vote in such House, is prevented from so sitting and voting by his Conscientious Objection to take the Oath which by an Act passed or to be passed in the present Session has been or may be substituted for the Oaths of Allegiance, Supremacy and Abjuration in the Form therein required, such House, if it think fit, may resolve that thenceforth any Person professing the Jewish Religion, in taking the same Oath to entitle him to sit and vote as aforesaid, may omit the Words "And I make this Declaration upon the True Faith of a Christian," and so long as such Resolution shall continue in force the said Oath taken and subscribed by any Person professing the Jewish Relgion to entitle him to sit and vote in that House of Parliament, may be modified accordingly; and the taking and subscribing by any Person professing the Jewish Religion of the Oath so modified shall, so far as respects the Title to sit and vote in such House, have the same Force and Effect as the taking and subscribing by other Persons of the said Oath in the Form required by the said Act.

II. In all other Cases, except for sitting in Parliament as aforesaid, or in qualifying to exercise the Right of Presentation to any Ecclesiastical Benefice in Scotland, whenever any of Her Majesty's Subjects professing the Jewish Religion shall be required to take the said Oath, the Words "And I make this Declaration upon the true faith of a Christian" shall be omitted.

III. Nothing herein contained shall extend or be construed to extend to enable any Person or Persons professing the Jewish Religion to hold or exercise the Office of Guardians and Justices of the United Kingdom, or of Regent of the United Kingdom, under whatever Names, Style, or Title, such Office may be constituted, or of Lord High Chancellor, Lord Keeper or Lord Commissioner of the Great Seal of Great Britain or Ireland, or the Office of Lord Lieutenant or Deputy or other Chief Governor or Governors of Ireland, or Her Majesty's High Commissioner to the General Assembly of the Church of Scotland.

IV. Any Right of Presentation to any Ecclesiastical Benefice shall belong to any Office in the Gift or Appointment of Her Majesty, Her Heirs, or Successors, and such Office shall be held by a Person professing the Jewish Religion, the Right of Presentation shall devolve upon and be exercised by the Archbishop of Canterbury for the Time being; and it shall not be lawful for any Person professing the Jewish Religion directly or indirectly, to advise Her Majesty, Her Heirs, or Successors, or any Person or Persons holding or exercising the Office of Guardians of the United Kingdom, or of Regent of the United Kingdom, under whatever Name, Style, or Title such Office may be constituted, or the Lord Lieutenant or Lord Deputy, or any Chief Governor or Governors of Ireland, touching or concerning the Appointment to or disposal of any Office or Preferment in the United Church of England and Ireland, or in the Church of Scotland: and if such Person shall offend in the Premises he shall, being thereof convicted by due Course of Law be deemed guilty of a high Misdemeanor, and disabled for ever from holding any Office, Civil or Military, under the Crown.

COBDEN TREATY OF COMMERCE WITH FRANCE, January 23, 1860

Source:　　The Annual Register, 1860. (London: Longman & Co., 1861)

In an effort to improve relations between France and Great
Britain, the Cobden Treaty was arranged. The British agreed to
admit French wines and liquors at an excise tax rate no higher
than that placed on British spirits. In return France was to grant
favorable treatment to British manufactured goods. The English
were to eventually have the greater advantage because of greater
French demand for their goods.

Treaty of Commerce Between Her Majesty and the Emperor of
the French.

Signed at Paris, January 23, 1860

Her Majesty the Queen of the United Kingdom of Great Britain and
Ireland, and His Majesty the Emperor of the French, being equally ani-
mated with the desire to draw closer the ties of friendship which unite
their two people, and wishing to improve and extend them between their
respective dominions, have resolved to conclude a Treaty for that purpose, and have named . . . Pleniopentiaries, . . .

Who, after having communicated to each other their respective
full powers, found in good and due form, have agreed upon and concluded
the following Articles:

I. His Majesty the Emperor of the French engages that on the following
articles of British production and manufacture, imported from the United
Kingdom into France, the duty shall in no case exceed thirty per cent,
ad valorem, . . . [List of articles follows.]

II. His Imperial Majesty engages to reduce the import duties in
France on British coal and coke, . . .
His Majesty the Emperor also engages, within four years from the
date of the ratification of the present Treaty to establish upon the importation of coal and coke by land and by sea, a uniform duty . . .

III. It is understood that the rates of duty mentioned in the preceding
Articles are independent of the differential duties in favor of French
shipping, with which duties they shall not interfere, ...

IV. Her Britannic Majesty engages to recommend to Parliament
to enable Her to abolish the duties of importation on the following articles: --- [List of articles follow] . . .

VI. Her Britannic Majesty engages also to propose to Parliament that the duties on the importation of French wines be at once reduced to a rate not exceeding three shillings a gallon, and that from the 1st April, 1861, the duties on importation shall be regulated as follows: --

1. On wines containing less than fifteen degrees of proof spirit . . . the duty shall not exceed one shilling a gallon.

2. On wine containing fifteen to twenty-six degrees, the duty shall not exceed one shilling and six pence a gallon.

3. On wine containing from twenty-six to forty degrees the duty shall not exceed two shillings a gallon.

4. On wine in bottles, the duty shall not exceed two shillings a gallon.

5. Wine shall not be imported at any other ports than those which shall be named for that purpose for the present Treaty shall come into force; Her Britannic reserving to Herself the right of substituting other ports for those which have been originally named, or of increasing the number of them. . . .

6. Her Britannic Majesty reserves to Herself the power notwithstanding the provisions of this article, to fix the maximum amount of proof spirit which may be contained in liquor declared as wine without, however, the maximum being lower than thirty-seven degrees. . . .

VIII. . . . Her Britannic Majesty undertakes to recommend to Parliament the admission into the United Kingdom of brandies and spirits imported from France, at a duty exactly equal to the Excise duty levied upon home-made spirits, with the addition of a surtax of two-pence a gallon, which will make the effectual duty payable on French brandies and spirits eight shillings and two pence a gallon. . . .

IX. It is understood between the two High Contracting Powers, that if one of them thinks it necessary to establish an Excise Tax or inland duty upon any article of home production or manufacture which is comprised on the preceding enumerated articles, the foreign imported articles of the same description may be immediately liable to an equivalent duty on importation.

It is equally understood between the High Contracting Parties that in case the British Government should deem it necessary to increase the Excise Duties levied upon home-made spirits, the duties on the importation of wines may be modified. . .

XI. The two High Contracting Parties engage not to prohibit the exportation of coal, and to levy no duty upon such exportation. . . .

XIX. Each of the two High Contracting Powers engage to confer on the other any favour, privilege, or reduction in the Tariff of Duties of importation on the articles mentioned in the present Treaty, which the said Power may concede to any third Power. They further engage not to enforce one against the other any prohibitions or importations or exportations which shall not at the same time be applicable to all other nations. . . .

XXII. The present Treaty shall be ratified, and the ratifications shall be exchanged at Paris within a period of fifteen days, or sooner if possible.

In faith whereof, the respective Plenipotentiaries have signed it, and affixed thereto the seal of their arms.

Done in duplicate at Paris, the twenty-third day of January, in the year of our Lord one thousand eight hundred and sixty.

(L.S.) Cowley
(L.S.) Richard Cobden
(L.S.) V. Baroche
(L.S.) F. Rouher

ROYAL TITLE -- EMPRESS OF INDIA, April 28, 1876

Source: The Annual Register, 1876 (London: Longman & Co., 1877)

In his efforts to improve the British position in the Empire
and advance the imperialist tradition, Benjamin Disraeli, leader
of the Conservative party and Prime Minister of Britain, obtained
passage of legislation in Parliament which created the title of
Empress of India for Queen Victoria. Disraeli had developed a
close relationship with the Queen and convinced her of the value
of this additional title. In addition he had the government play a
more active role in the determination of policy of the overseas
territories. The proclamation of the Queen's new title follows.

Proclamation of the Queen's New Title

Victoria R. --

Whereas an Act has been passed in the Present Session of Parliament, intituled "An Act to enable Her Most Gracious Majesty to make
an Addition to the Royal Style and Title appertaining to the Imperial
Crown of the United Kingdom and its Dependencies," which Act recites
that, by the Act for the Union of Great Britain and Ireland, it was provided
that after such Union the Royal Style and Title appertaining to the Imperial Crown of the United Kingdom and its Dependencies should be
such that His Majesty by His Royal Proclamation under the Great Seal
of the United Kingdom should be pleased to appoint; and which Act also
recites that by virtue of said Act and the Royal Proclamation under the
Great Seal, dated the 1st day of January 1801, our present Style and
Title are "Victoria, by the Grace of God, of the United Kingdom of Great
Britain and Ireland, Queen, Defender of the Faith;" and which Act also
recites that, by the Act for the Better Government of India it was enacted
that the government of India, theretofor vested in the East India Company
in trust for Us should become vested in Us, and that India should thenceforth be governed by Us and in Our Name, and that it is expedient that
there should be a recognition of the transfer of Government so made by
means of an addition to be made to Our Style and Titles: and which Act,
after the said recitals, enacts that is shall be lawful for Us, with a view
to such recognition as aforesaid, of the transfer of the Government of
India, by Our Royal Proclamation under the Great Seal of the United Kingdom, to make such addition to the Style and Title at present appertaining
to the Imperial Crown of the United Kingdom and its Dependencies as to Us
may seem meet; We have thought fit, by and with the advice of Our Privy
Council, to appoint and declare, and We do hereby, by and with the said
advice appoint and declare that henceforth so far as conveniently may be,
on all occasions and in all instruments wherein our Style and Titles are
used, save and exempt all Charters, Commisions, Letters Patent, Grants,

Writs, Appointments, and other like instruments, not extending in their operation beyond the United Kingdom, the following addition shall be made to the Style and Titles at present appertaining to the Imperial Crown of the United Kingdom of Great Britain and her Dependencies: that is to say, in the Latin tongue in these words "Indiae Imperatrix." and in the English tongue in these words, "Empress of India."

And Our will and Pleasure further is, that the said addition shall be made in the Commissions, Charters, Letters Patent, Grants, Writs, Appointments, and other like Instruments hereinbefore specifically accepted.

And Our Will and Pleasure further is, . . . that all gold, silver, and copper moneys shall on or after this day, be coined for Our authority with the like impressions, shall notwithstanding such addition to Our Style and Titles, be deemed and taken to be current and lawful moneys for and issued in any of the Dependencies of the said United Kingdom and declared by Our Proclamation to be current and lawful money of such Dependencies respectively bearing Our Style or Title, or any part or parts thereof, and all moneys which shall hereafter be coined and issued according to such Proclamation, shall notwithstanding such addition, continue to be lawful and current money of such Dependencies respectively, until Our Pleasure shall be further declared thereupon.

Given at Our Court at Windsor the twenty-eighth day of April one thousand eight hundred and seventy-six in the thirty-ninth year of Our Reign.

God Save the Queen.

STATUTE OF WESTMINSTER, December 11, 1931

Source: The Public General Acts and . . . Measures of 1931. (London, 1932)

The Dominions of Canada and New Zealand, the Commonwealth of Australia, the Union of South Africa, the Irish Free State, and Newfoundland sent representatives to meet at Westminster for a series of Imperial Conferences in 1926 and 1930. They adopted several proposals which were enacted in the following statute. From 1931 on the various Dominions were to enact their own legislation. This was the first step leading to the creation of the Commonwealth of Nations.

An Act to give effect to certain resolutions passed by Imperial Conferences held in the years 1926 and 1930

[11 December 1931]

WHEREAS the delegates of His Majesty's Governments in the United Kingdom, the Dominion of Canada, the Commonwealth of Australia, the Dominion of New Zealand, the Union of South Africa, the Irish Free State and Newfoundland, at Imperial Conferences holden at Westminster in the years of our Lord nineteen hundred and twenty-six and nineteen hundred and thirty did concur in making the declarations and resolutions set forth in the Reports of the said Conferences:

And whereas it is meet and proper to set out by way of preamble to this Act that, inasmuch as the Crown is the symbol of the free association of the members of the British Commonwealth of Nations, and as they are united by a common allegiance to the Crown, it would be in accord with the established constitutional position of all the members of the Commonwealth in relation to one another that any alteration in the law touching the Succession to the Throne or the Royal Style and Titles shall hereafter require the assent as well of the Parliaments of all the Dominions as of the Parliament of the United Kingdom:

And whereas it is in accord with the established constitutional position that no law hereafter made by the Parliament of the United Kingdom shall extend to any of the said Dominions as part of the law of that Dominion otherwise than at the request and with the consent of that Dominion:

And whereas it is necessary for the ratifying, confirming and establishing of certain of the said declarations and resolutions of the said Conferences that a law be made and enacted in due form by authority of the Parliament of the United Kingdom:

And whereas the Dominion of Canada, the Commonwealth of Australia, the Dominion of New Zealand, the Union of South Africa, the Irish Free State and Newfoundland have severally requested and consented to the submission of a measure to the Parliament of the United Kingdom for making such provision with regard to the matters aforesaid as is here-after in this Act contained:

Now, therefore, be it enacted by the King's most Excellent Majesty by and with the advice and consent of the Lords Spiritual and Temporal, and Commons, in this present Parliament assembled, and by the authority of the same, as follows:

1. In this Act the expression 'Dominion' means any of the following Dominions, that is to say, the Dominion of Canada, the Commonwealth of Australia, the Dominion of New Zealand, the Union of South Africa, the Irish Free State and Newfoundland.

2. -- (1) The Colonial Laws Validity Act, 1865, shall not apply to any law made after the commencement of this Act by the Parliament of a Dominion.

(2) No law and no provision of any law made after the commencement of this Act by the Parliament of a Dominion shall be void or inoperative on the ground that it is repugnant to the law of England, or to the provisions of any existing or future Act of Parliament of the United Kingdom, or to any order, rule or regulation made under any such Act, and the powers of the Parliament of a Dominion shall include the power to repeal or amend any such Act, order, rule or regulation in so far as the same is part of the law of the Dominion.

3. It is hereby declared and enacted that the Parliament of a Dominion has full power to make laws having extra-territorial operation.

4. No Act of Parliament of the United Kingdom passed after the commencement of this Act shall extend, or be deemed to extend, to a Dominion as part of the law of that Dominion, unless it is expressly declared in that Act that that Dominion has requested, and consented to, the enactment thereof.

5. Without prejudice to the generality of the foregoing provisions of this Act, sections seven hundred and thirty-five and seven hundred and thirty-six of the Merchant Shipping Act, 1894, shall be construed as though reference therein to the Legislature of a British possession did not include reference to the Parliament of a Dominion.

6. Without prejudice to the generality of the foregoing provisions of this Act, section four of the Colonial Courts of Admiralty Act, 1890 (which requires certain laws to be reserved for the signification of His Majesty's pleasure or to contain a suspending clause), and so much of section seven of that Act as requires the approval of His Majesty in Council to any rules of Court for regulating the practice and procedure of a Colonial Court of Admiralty, shall cease to have effect in any Dominion as from the commencement of this Act.

*   *   *

ANGLO-POLISH MUTUAL ASSISTANCE PACT, August 25, 1939

Source: British and Foreign State Papers, 1939. (London: His Majesty's
Stationery Office, 1951) Vol. 143, pp. 301-303.

Following the dismemberment of Czechoslovakia by the Germans, the United Kingdom decided to negotiate a treaty of mutual
assistance with the Polish government in the event of an attack
by Nazi Germany. Under the stipulations of this agreement
if either party were attacked the other would come to its aid. The
Treaty was to remain in force for five years. It went into effect
when Germany invaded Poland.

AGREEMENT OF MUTUAL ASSISTANCE between the United Kingdom
    and Poland. -- London, August 25, 1939

THE Government of the United Kingdom of Great Britain and Northern
Ireland and the Polish Government:
    Desiring to place on a permanent basis the collaboration between
their respective countries resulting from the assurances of mutual assistance of a defensive character which they have already exchanged;
    Have resolved to conclude an agreement for that purpose and have
appointed as their plenipotentiaries:
                     [Here follow the names]
    Who, having exchanged their full powers, found in good and due
form, have agreed on the following provisions: --
    ART. 1. Should one of the contracting parties become engaged in
hostilities with a European power in consequence of aggression by the
latter against that contracting party, the other contracting party will at
once give the contracting party engaged in hostilities all the support and
assistance in its power.
    2. -- (1) The provisions of article 1 will also apply in the event
of any action by a European power which clearly threatened, directly
or indirectly, the independence of one of the contracting parties, and
was of such a nature that the party in question considered it vital to
resist it with its armed forces.
    (2) Should one of the contracting parties become engaged
in hostilities with a European power in consequence of action by that
power which threatened the independence or neutrality of another European
state in such a way as to constitute a clear menace to the security of
that contracting party, the provisions of article 1 will apply, without
prejudice, however, to the rights of the other European state concerned.
    3. Should a European power attempt to undermine the independence
of one of the contracting parties by process of economic penetration or in
any other way, the contracting parties support each other in resistance
to such attempts. Should the European power concerned thereupon embark
on hostilities against one of the contracting parties, the provisions of

article 1 will apply.

4. The methods of applying the undertakings of mutual assistance provided for by the present agreement are established between the competent naval, military and air authorities of the contracting parties.

5. Without prejudice to the foregoing undertakings of the contracting parties to give each other mutual support and assistance immediately on the outbreak of hostilities, they will exchange complete and speedy information concerning any development which might threaten their independence and, in particular, concerning any development which threatened to call the said undertakings into operation.

6. -- (1) The contracting parties will communicate to each other the terms of any undertakings of assistance against aggression which they have already given or may in future give to other states.

(2) Should either of the contracting parties intend to give such an undertaking after the coming into force of the present agreement, the other contracting party shall, in order to ensure the proper functioning of the agreement, be informed thereof.

(3) Any new undertaking which the contracting parties may enter into in future shall neither limit their obligations under the present agreement nor indirectly create new obligations between the contracting party not participating in these undertakings and the third state concerned.

7. Should the contracting parties be engaged in hostilities in consequence of the application of the present agreement, they will not conclude an armistice or treaty of peace except by mutual agreement.

8. -- (1) The present agreement shall remain in force for a period of 5 years.

(2) Unless denounced 6 months before the expiry of this period it shall continue in force, each contracting party having thereafter the right to denounce it at any time by giving 6 months' notice to that effect.

(3) The present agreement shall come into force on signature.

In faith whereof the above-named plenipotentiaries have signed the present agreement and have affixed thereto their seals.

Done in English in duplicate, at London, the 25th August, 1939. A Polish text shall subsequently be agreed upon between the contracting parties and both texts will then be authentic.

(L.S.)   HALIFAX.
(L.S.)   EDWARD RACZYNSKI.

LEND LEASE AGREEMENT, March 27, 1941

Source: British and Foreign State Papers, 1940-42. (London: His Majesty's Stationery Office, 1952) Vol. 144, pp. 645-683.

When Great Britain and Germany went into war, the United States was limited under its Neutrality Legislation in the amount and type of goods which it could sell to the belligerents. In order to get around this limitation, President Franklin D. Roosevelt and Prime Minister Winston Churchill arranged for their governments the lease of British bases to the United States in return for the lending of over-age destroyers by the United States to Britain.

AGREEMENT between the United Kingdom and the United States of America relating to the Bases leased to the United States of America and Exchanges of Notes together with Protocol between the United Kingdom, Canada and the United States of America concerning the Defence of Newfoundland. -- London, March 27, 1941

No. 1

WHEREAS the Government of the United Kingdom of Great Britain and Northern Ireland, in consultation with the Government of Newfoundland, are desirous at this time of further effectuating the declarations made on their behalf by his Excellency the Most Honourable the Marquess of Lothian, C. H., His Majesty's Ambassador Extraordinary and Plenipotentiary, in his communication of the 2nd September, 1940, to the Secretary of State of the United States of America, . . .

And whereas it is agreed that leases in respect of the naval and air bases to be leased to the United States of America in Newfoundland, Bermuda, Jamaica, St. Lucia, Antigua, Trinidad and British Guiana, respectively, shall forthwith be executed substantially in the forms of the leases set out in Annex II hereto, which are hereby approved, and that a similar lease in respect of a base in the Bahamas shall be executed as soon as possible;

And whereas it is desired to determine by common agreement certain matters relating to the lease of the said bases, as provided in the communication of the 2nd September, 1940, and the reply thereto of the same date from the Honourable Cordell Hull, Secretary of State of the United States, set out in Annex I and made a part hereof;

And whereas it is desired that this Agreement shall be fulfilled in a spirit of good neighbourliness between the Government of the United Kingdom and the Government of the United States of America, and that details of its practical application shall be arranged by friendly co-operation;

The Undersigned, duly authorised to that effect, have agreed as follows: --

General Description of Rights

ART. 1. -- (1) The United States shall have all the rights, power and authority within the Leased Areas which are necessary for the establishment, use, operation and defence thereof, or appropriate for their control, and all the rights, power and authority within the limits of territorial waters and air spaces adjacent to, or in the vicinity of, the Leased Areas, which are necessary to provide access to and defence of the Leased Areas, or appropriate for control thereof.

(2) The said rights, power and authority shall include, inter alia, the right, power and authority: --

(a) to construct (including dredging and filling), maintain, operate, use, occupy and control the said Bases;

(b) to improve and deepen the harbours, channels, entrances and anchorages, and generally to fit the premises for use as naval and air bases;

(c) to control, so far as may be required for the efficient operation of the Bases, and within the limits of military necessity, anchorages, moorings and movements of ships and waterborne craft and the anchorages, moorings, landings, takeoffs, movements and operations of aircraft;

(d) to regulate and control within the Leased Areas all communications within, to and from the areas leased;

(e) to install, maintain, use and operate under-sea and other defences, defence devices and controls, including detecting and other similar facilities.

(3) In the exercise of the above-mentioned rights, the United States agrees that the powers granted to it outside the Leased Areas will not be used unreasonably or, unless required by military necessity, so as to interfere with the necessary rights of navigation, aviation or communication to or from or within the Territories, but that they shall be used in the spirit of the fourth clause of the Preamble.

(4) In the practical application outside the Leased Areas of the foregoing paragraphs there shall be, as occasion requires, consultation between the Government of the United States and the Government of the United Kingdom.

Special Emergency Powers

2. When the United States is engaged in war or in time of other emergency, the Government of the United Kingdom agree that the United States may exercise in the Territories and surrounding waters or air spaces all such rights, power and authority as may be necessary for conducting any military operations deemed desirable by the United States, but these rights will be exercised with all possible regard to the spirit of the fourth clause of the Preamble.

Non-user

3. The United States shall be under no obligation to improve the Leased Areas or any part thereof for use as naval or air bases, or to

exercise any right, power or authority granted in respect of the Leased Areas, or to maintain forces therein, or to provide for the defence thereof; but if and so long as any Leased Area, or any part thereof, is not used by the United States for the purposes in this Agreement set forth, the Government of the United Kingdom or the Government of the Territory may take such steps therein as shall be agreed with the United States to be desirable for the maintenance of public health, safety, law and order, and, if necessary, for defence.

*   *   *

LABOR LEGISLATION: NATIONAL HEALTH SERVICE ACT
November 6, 1946

Source: The Public General Acts and . . . Measures of 1946. (London:
His Majesty's Stationery Office, 1947) pp. 1119-1214.

The Labour party had recognized the problems involved in
providing medical services to the nation, especially after the de-
vastation of the Second World War. As a result the government
prepared a comprehensive scheme of health protection including
hospital, medical, dental, pharmaceutical and opthalmic services. The following selections from this act indicate the breadth
of the program.

1946 CHAPTER 81

An Act to provide for the establishment of a comprehensive health service
for England and Wales, and for purposes connected therewith. [6th
November 1946.]

Be it enacted by the King's most Excellent Majesty, by and with
the advice and consent of the Lords Spiritual and Temporal, and Commons,
in this present Parliament assembled, and by the authority of the same,
as follows: --

PART I.

CENTRAL ADMINISTRATION.

1. -- (I) It shall be the duty of the Minister of Health (hereafter
in this Act referred to as "the Minister") to promote the establishment
in England and Wales of a comprehensive health service designed to
secure improvement in the physical and mental health of the people of
England and Wales, and the prevention, diagnosis and treatment of illness,
and for that purpose to provide or secure the effective provision of services in accordance with the following provisions of this Act.
(2) The services so provided shall be free of charge, except where
any provision of this Act expressly provides for the making and recovery
of charges.
2. -- (I) There shall be constituted in accordance with the First
Schedule to this Act a council, to be called the Central Health Services
Council and hereafter in this Act referred to as "the Central Council",
and it shall be the duty of the Central Council to advise the Minister
upon such general matters relating to the services provided under this
Act, or any services provided by local health authorities in their capacity
as such authorities, as the Council think fit and upon any questions referred to them by him relating to those services.

(2) The Minister may, after consultation with the Central Council, by order vary the constitution of that Council.

(3) The Minister may, after consultation with the Central Council, by order constitute standing advisory committees for the purpose of advising him and the Central Council on such of the services aforesaid as may be specified in the order, and any committee constituted under this subsection shall consist partly of members of the Central Council appointed by the Minister after consultation with that Council of persons, whether members of the Central Council or not, appointed by the Minister after consultation with such representative organisations as the Minister may recognise for the purpose.

(4) It shall be the duty of a standing advisory committee constituted under this section to advise the Minister and the Central Council upon such matters relating to the services with which the committee are concerned as they think fit and upon any questions referred to them by the Minister or Central Council relating to those services, and, if the committee advise the Minister upon any matter, they shall inform the Central Council, who may express their views thereon to the Minister.

(5) The Central Council shall make an annual report to the Minister on their proceedings and on the proceedings of any standing advisory committee constituted under this section, and the Minister shall lay that report before Parliament with such comments (if any) as he thinks fit:

Provided that, if the Minister, after consultation with the Central Council, is satisfied that it would be contrary to the public interest to lay any such report, or a part of any such report, before Parliament, he may refrain from laying that report or part.

(6) The supplementary provisions contained in the First Schedule to this Act shall have effect in relation to the Central council and any standing advisory committee constituted under this section.

PART II.

HOSPITAL AND SPECIALIST SERVICES.

Provision of Services by Minister

3. -- (I) As from the appointed day, it shall be the duty of the Minister to provide throughout England and Wales, to such extent as he considers necessary to meet all reasonable requirements, accommodation and services of the following descriptions, that is to say: --

    (a) hospital accommodation;

    (b) medical, nursing and other services required at or for the purposes of hospitals;

    (c) the services of specialists, whether at a hospital, a health centre provided under Part III of this Act or a clinic or, if necessary on medical grounds, at the home of the patient;

and any accommodation and services provided under this section are in this Act referred to as "hospital and specialist services".

(2) Regulations may provide for the making and recovery by the Minister of such charges as may be prescribed --

(a) in respect of the supply, as part of the hospital and specialist services, of any appliance which is, at the request of the person supplied, of a more expensive type than the prescribed type, or in respect of the replacement or repair of any such appliance; or

(b) in respect of the replacement or repair of any appliance supplied as part of the services aforesaid, if it is determined in the prescribed manner that the replacement or repair is necessitated by lack of care on the part of the person supplied.

*   *   *

General Medical Services.

33. — (I) It shall be the duty of every Executive Council in accordance with the regulations to make as respects their areas arrangements with medical practitioners for the provision by them as from the appointed day, whether at a health centre or otherwise, of personal medical services for all persons in the area who wish to take advantage of the arrangements, and the services provided in accordance with the arrangements are in this Act referred to as "general medical services."

(2) Regulations may make provision for defining the personal medical services to be provided and for securing that the arrangements will be such that all persons availing themselves of those services will receive adequate personal care and attendance, and the regulations shall include provision —

(a) for the preparation and publication of lists of medical practitioners who undertake to provide general medical services;

(b) for conferring a right on any person to choose, in accordance with the prescribed procedure, the medical practitioner by whom he is to be attended, subject to the consent of the practitioner so chosen and to any prescribed limit on the number of patients to be accepted by any practitioner;

(c) for the distribution among medical practitioners whose names are on the lists of any persons who have indicated a wish to obtain general medical services but who have not made any choice of medical practitioner or have been refused by the practitioner chosen;

(d) for the issue to patients or their personal representatives by medical practitioners providing such services as aforesaid of certificates reasonably required by them under or for the purposes of any enactment.

*   *   *

Pharmaceutical Services, General Dental Services and Supplementary Ophthalmic Services.

38. — (I) It shall be the duty of every Executive Council in accordance with regulations to make as respects their area arrangements for the

supply as from the appointed day, whether at a health centre or otherwise, of proper and sufficient drugs and medicines and prescribed appliances to all persons in the area who are receiving general medical services, and of prescribed drugs and medicines to all persons in the area who are receiving general dental services, and the services provided in accordance with the arrangements are in this Act referred to as "pharmaceutical services".

(2) Regulations may make provision for securing that arrangements made under this section will be such as to enable any person receiving general medical services to obtain proper and sufficient drugs and medicines and prescribed appliances, if ordered by the medical practitioner rendering those services, from any persons with whom arrangements have been made under this section, and to enable any person receiving general dental services to obtain prescribed drugs and medicines, if ordered by the dental practitioner rendering those services, from any persons with whom such arrangements have been made, and the regulations shall include provision --

(a) for the preparation and publication of lists of persons who undertake to provide pharmaceutical services; and

(b) for conferring a right, subject to the provisions of this Part of this Act relating to the disqualification of practitioners, on any person who wishes to be included in any such list to be so included for the purpose of supplying such drugs, medicines and appliances as that person is entitled by law to sell.

*   *   *

LABOR LEGISLATION: NATIONALIZATION OF THE COAL INDUSTRY
November 6, 1946.

Source: The Public General Acts and . . . Measures of 1945. (London:
His Majesty's Stationery Office, 1946) pp. 399-468.

The Samuel Commission which had studied the coal industry
in the 1920's had recognized the difficulties and problems of the
coal mines at that time and had urged the necessity of some degree of governmental control. The Labour party had pledged as
part of its campaign platform in 1945 that it would nationalize
this industry and proceed to do so under this act creating
a National Coal Board to supervise the industry.

1945 CHAPTER 59

An Act to establish public ownership and control of the coal-mining industry
and certain allied activities; and for purposes connected therewith.
(12th July 1946.)

Be it enacted by the King's most Excellent Majesty, by and with the
advice and consent of the Lords Spiritual and Temporal, and Commons,
in this present Parliament assembled, and by the authority of the same,
as follows: --

The National Coal Board.

1. -- (I) There shall be a National Coal Board which shall, on
and after the primary vesting date, be charged with the duties of --
  (a) working and getting the coal in Great Britain, to the ex-
      clusion (save as in this Act provided) of any other person;
  (b) securing the efficient development of the coal-mining in-
      dustry; and
  (c) making supplies of coal available, of such qualities and
      sizes, in such quantities and at such prices, as may seem
      to them best calculated to further the public interest in all
      respects, including the avoidance of any undue or unreasonable
      preference or advantage.
  (2) The functions of the National Coal Board (in this Act referred to
as "the Board") shall include the carrying on of all such activities as
it may appear to the Board to be requisite, advantageous or convenient
for them to carry on for or in connection with the discharge of their
duties under the preceding subsection, and in particular, but without
prejudice to the generality of this section, --
  (a) searching and boring for coal in Great Britain, to the ex-
      clusion of any other person;
  (b) treating, rendering saleable, supplying and selling coal;

(c) producing, manufacturing, treating, rendering saleable, supplying and selling products of coal;

(d) producing or manufacturing any goods or utilities which are of a kind required by the Board for or in connection with the working and getting of coal or any other of their activities, of which can advantageously be produced or manufactured by the Board by reason of their having materials or facilities for the production or manufacture of coal or any other of their activities, and supplying and selling goods or utilities so produced or manufactured;

(e) any activities which can advantageously be carried on by the Board with a view to making the best use of any of the assets vested in them by this Act;

(f) activities conducive to advancing the skill of persons employed or to be employed for the purposes of any of the activities aforesaid, or the efficiency of equipment and methods to be used therefor, including the provision by the Board themselves, and their assisting the provision by others, of facilities for training, education and research.

(3) The Board shall have power to do any thing and to enter into any transaction (whether or not involving the expenditure, borrowing in accordance with the provisions of this Act in that behalf or lending of money, the acquisition of any property or rights, or the disposal of any property or rights not in their opinion required for the proper discharge of their functions) which in their opinion is calculated to facilitate the proper discharge of their duties under subsection (I) of this section or the carrying on by them of any such activities as aforesaid, or is incidental or conducive thereto.

(4) The policy of the Board shall be directed to securing, consistently with the proper discharge of their duties under subsection (I) of this section, --

(a) the safety, health and welfare of persons in their employment;

(b) the benefit of the practical knowledge and experience of such persons in the organisation and conduct of the operations in which they are employed;

(c) that the revenues of the Board shall not be less than sufficient for meeting all their outgoings properly chargeable to revenue account (including, without prejudice to the generality of that expression, provisions in respect of their obligations under sections twenty-eight and twenty-nine of this Act) on an average of good and bad years.

2. --(I) The Board shall be a body corporate by the name of "the National Coal Board", which perpetual succession and a common seal and power to hold land without licence in mortmain.

*　　　　　*　　　　　*

ESTABLISHMENT OF INDIA AND PAKISTAN, July 18, 1947

Source: The Public General Acts and . . . Measures of 1947. (London,
1955) Part I, pp. 158-177.

The British had been negotiating with the Indians for the establishment of an independent state within the Commonwealth.
The differences between the Hindus and the Moslems were so
great that the final solution on the part of the British government
was to create two separate states: India and Pakistan. The following act provided for the establishment of these two nations.

ACT OF PARLIAMENT to make provision for the setting up in India
of two independent Dominions, to substitute other provisions for
certain provisions of the Government of India Act, 1935, which
apply outside those Dominions, and to provide for other matters
consequential on or connected with the setting up of those Dominions

(10 & 11 Geo. 6. c. 30)   (July 18, 1947)
BE it enacted by the King's most Excellent Majesty, by and with
the advice and consent of the Lords Spiritual and Temporal, and Commons, in this present Parliament assembled, and by the authority of the
same, as follows: --

1. -- (1) As from the 15th day of August, 1947, two independent
Dominions shall be set up in India, to be known respectively as India
and Pakistan.

(2) The said Dominions are hereafter in this Act referred
to as "the new Dominions", and the said 15th day of August is hereafter in this Act referred to as "the appointed day".

2. -- (1) Subject to the provisions of sub-sections (3) and (4) of
this section, the territories of India shall be the territories under the
sovereignty of His Majesty which, immediately before the appointed day,
were included in British India except the territories which, under sub-
section (2) of this section, are to be the territories of Pakistan.

(2) Subject to the provisions of sub-sections (3) and (4) of
this section, the territories of Pakistan shall be --

(a) the territories which, on the appointed day, are included in
the Provinces of East Bengal and West Punjab, as constituted
under the two following sections;

(b) the territories which, at the date of the passing of this Act,
are included in the Province of Sind and the Chief Commissioner's Province of British Baluchistan; and

(c) if, whether before or after the passing of this Act but before
the appointed day, the Governor-General declares that the
majority of the valid votes cast in the referendum which, at
the date of the passing of this Act, is being or has recently

been held in that behalf under his authority in the North West Frontier Province are in favour of representatives of that Province taking part in the Constituent Assembly of Pakistan, the territories which, at the date of the passing of this Act, are included in that Province.

(3) Nothing in this section shall prevent any area being at any time included in or excluded from either of the new Dominions, so, however, that --

(a) no area not forming part of the territories specified in sub-section (1) or, as the case may be, sub-section (2), of this section shall be included in either Dominion without the consent of that Dominion; and

(b) no area which forms part of the territories specified in the said sub-section (1) or, as the case may be, the said sub-section (2), or which has after the appointed day been included in either Dominion, shall be excluded from that Dominion without the consent of that Dominion.

(4) Without prejudice to the generality of the provisions of sub-section (3) of this section, nothing in this section shall be construed as preventing the accession of Indian States to either of the new Dominions.

3. -- (1) As from the appointed day --

(a) the Province of Bengal, as constituted under the Government of India Act, 1935, shall cease to exist; and

(b) there shall be constituted in lieu thereof two new Provinces, to be known respectively as East Bengal and West Bengal.

(2) If, whether before or after the passing of this Act, but before the appointed day, the Governor-General declares that the majority of the valid votes cast in the referendum which, at the date of the passing of this Act, is being or has recently been held in that behalf under his authority in the District of Sylhet are in favour of that District forming part of the new Province of East Bengal, then, as from that day, a part of the Province of Assam shall, in accordance with the provisions of sub-section (3) of this section, form part of the new Province of East Bengal.

*   *   *

ELECTRICITY ACT, August 13, 1947

Source: The Public General Acts and . . . Measures of 1947. (London:
His Majesty's Stationery Office, 1947) pp. 1809-1932.

The Labour government found it necessary to assume control of the utilities in order to provide efficient electric service
at reasonable costs to the nation so that it might go on with the
important work of reconstruction after the war. Selections from
the act as printed below illustrate the type of governmental control involved.

1947 CHAPTER 54

An Act to provide for the establishment of a British Electricity Authority
and Area Electricity Boards and for the exercise and performance
by that Authority and those Boards and the North of Scotland Hydro-
Electric Board of functions relating to the supply of electricity
and certain other matters; for the transfer to the said Authority
or any such Board as aforesaid of property, rights, obligations and
liabilities of electricity undertakers and other bodies; to amend
the law relating to the supply of electricity; to make certain consequential provision as to income tax; and for purposes connected
with the matters aforesaid.

[13th August 1947.]

Be it enacted by the King's most Excellent Majesty, by and with
the advice and consent of the Lords Spiritual and Temporal, and Commons, in this present Parliament assembled, and by the authority of
the same, as follows: --

PART I.

BRITISH ELECTRICITY AUTHORITY AND AREA
ELECTRICITY BOARDS.

1. -- (1) There shall be established an Authority, to be known as
the British Electricity Authority, and it shall be the duty of that Authority
as from the vesting date to develop and maintain an efficient, co-ordinated
and economical system of electricity supply for all parts of Great Britain
except the North of Scotland District, and for that purpose --
    (a) to generate or acquire supplies of electricity;
    (b) to provide bulk supplies of electricity for the Area Boards
        hereinafter established for distribution by those Boards;
    (c) to co-ordinate the distribution of electricity by Area Boards
        and to exercise a general control over the policy of those
        Boards; and

(d) to provide supplies of electricity for consumers for whom the British Electricity Authority are required by any provision of this Act or may for the time being be authorised by the Minister to provide such supplies.

(2) There shall be established Boards, to be known by the names mentioned in the first column of the First Schedule to this Act, for the areas which are described in general terms in the second column of that Schedule and are to be defined by orders made under this Part of this Act, and it shall be the duty of every such Board as from the vesting date to acquire from the British Electricity Authority bulk supplies of electricity and to plan and carry out an efficient and economical distribution of those supplies to persons in their area who require them.

*   *   *

(6) In exercising and performing their functions the Electricity Boards shall, subject to and in accordance with any directions given by the Minister or Secretary of State under this Part of this Act --

(a) promote the use of all economical methods of generating, transmitting and distributing electricity;

(b) secure, so far as practicable, the development, extension to rural areas and cheapening of supplies of electricity;

(c) avoid undue preferences in the provision of such supplies;

(d) promote the simplification and standardisation of methods of charge for such supplies;

(3) promote the standardisation of systems of supply and types of electrical fittings;

and shall also promote the welfare, health and safety of persons in the employment of the Boards.

*   *   *

PALESTINE ACT, April 29, 1948

Source: The Public General Acts and . . . Measures of 1948. (London: His Majesty's Stationery Office, 1948) pp. 218-222.

As a result of the recommendation of the United Nations, the United Kingdom determined to end their mandate in respect to Palestine by May 15, 1948. The following selections from the Act indicate the manner in which the British would terminate their control.

1948 CHAPTER 27.

An Act to make provision with respect to the termination of His Majesty's jurisdiction in Palestine, and for purposes connected therewith.
[29th April 1948.]

Be it enacted by the King's most Excellent Majesty, by and with the advice and consent of the Lords Spiritual and Temporal, and Commons, in this present Parliament assembled, and by the authority of the same, as follows: --

1. -- (1) On the fifteenth day of May, nineteen hundred and forty-eight, or such earlier date as His Majesty may by Order in Council declare to be the date on which the mandate in respect of Palestine accepted by His Majesty on behalf of the League of Nations will be relinquished (in this Act referred to as "the appointed day"), all jurisdiction of His Majesty in Palestine shall determine, and His Majesty's Government in the United Kingdom shall cease to be responsible for the government of Palestine.

(2) Nothing in this Act shall affect the jurisdiction of His Majesty, or any powers of the Admiralty, the Army Council or the Air Council, or of any other authority, in relation to any of His Majesty's forces which may be in Palestine on or after the appointed day.

2. -- (1) Any appeal to His Majesty in Council which, on the appointed day, is pending from any court in Palestine, not being a prize court constituted under the Prize Acts, 1864 to 1944, shall abate on that day.

(2) No proceeding, whether civil or criminal, shall be instituted in any court to which this subsection applies in respect of anything done, whether within or outside Palestine, by any person in the service of His Majesty or by any person acting under the authority of any such person, if done in good faith and done or purported to be done in the execution of his duty --

    (a) before the appointed day, for the maintenance of peace or order in Palestine, or otherwise for the good government thereof;

(b) whether before, on or after that day, for the purpose of or in connection with the termination of His Majesty's juris- diction in Palestine or the withdrawal from Palestine of any of His Majesty's forces or of any stores or other property belonging to His Majesty or to any such forces, or the pro- tection of any such forces, stores or property; or

(c) on or after that day and before the withdrawal from Palestine of the said forces, for the protection in Palestine of the life or property of any British subject:

Provided that nothing in this subsection shall prevent the institution of any proceedings in respect of anything done before the twenty-sixth day of February, nineteen hundred and forty-eight, or the institution of any proceedings on behalf of His Majesty.

(3) The courts to which the last foregoing subsection applies are British courts, not being courts martial, exercising jurisdiction either within or outside the United Kingdom, except courts in a Dominion, in Southern Rhodesia, or in any territory administered by the govern- ment of a Dominion.

(4) For the purposes of this section, a certificate by a Sec- retary of State or the Admiralty that anything was done under the authority of a person in the service of His Majesty, or was done by any person in the execution of his duty, shall be sufficient evidence of the matter so certified; and anything done by or under the authority of a person in the service of His Majesty shall be deemed to have been done in good faith unless the contrary is proved.

(5) In this section the expression "Dominion" means a Dominion within the meaning of the Statute of Westminster, 1931, India, Pakistan and Ceylon; and references in this section to anything done shall be con- strued as including references to anything omitted to be done.

*   *   *

(4) His Majesty may by Order in Council make provision --
(a) for the disposal or application of any property vested in or belonging to the Government of Palestine or any public authority constituted under any law in force in Palestine before the appointed day;
(b) for applying any enactment relating to superannuation, in relation to any person who holds office in the service of the Government of Palestine immediately before the appointed day, as if he continued to hold office during such period after that day as may be determined by or under the Order;
(c) for any other purpose which appears to His Majesty to be necessary or expedient in consequence of the termination of his jurisdiction in Palestine.

4. -- (1) Any Order in Council made under the last foregoing section after the appointed day may be made so as to take effect as from that day or as from such later date as may be specified therein.

(2) Any Order in Council made under the last foregoing section may be varied or revoked by a subsequent Order in Council. . . .

THE TELEVISION ACT, July 30, 1954

Source: The Public General Acts and . . . Measures of 1954. (London:
Her Majesty's Stationery Office, 1954) pp. 481-502.

As in the case of radio broadcasting, the British government
had decided that it would be in the best interests of the government to have the British Broadcasting Corporation develop the
television industry and to broadcast without advertisements
through grants provided by the government. In 1954 the government decided to establish an Independent Television Authority which would be permitted to sell broadcast time to interested
sponsors. The following selections from the act indicate the matter of regulation of this authority.

1954 CHAPTER 55

An Act to make provision for television broadcasting services in ad-
    dition to those provided by the British Broadcasting Corporation,
    and to set up a special authority for that purpose; to make pro-
    vision as to the constitution, powers, duties and financial resources
    of that authority and as to the position and obligations of persons
    contracting with that authority for the provision of programmes
    and parts of programmes; and for purposes connected with the
    matters aforesaid.

[30th July, 1954]

Be it enacted by the Queen's most Excellent Majesty, by and with
the advice and consent of the Lords Spiritual and Temporal, and Commons, in this present Parliament assembled, and by the authority of the
same, as follows: --

1. -- (1) There shall be an authority, to be called the Independent
Television Authority (in this Act referred to as "the Authority") whose
function shall be to provide, in accordance with the provisions of this
Act, and for the period of ten years from the passing of this Act, television broadcasting services, additional to those of the British Broadcasting Corporation and of high quality, both as to the transmission and
as to the matter transmitted, for so much of the United Kingdom, the Isle
of Man and the Channel Islands as may from time to time be reasonably
practicable.

(2) The Authority shall consist of a Chairman, a Deputy
Chairman and such other members, not being less than five nor more
than eight, as the Postmaster-General may from time to time determine:
Provided that unless and until the Postmaster-General otherwise
determines by notice in writing to the Authority, a copy of which shall
be laid before each House of Parliament, the number of the said other

members shall be eight.

(3) All the members of the Authority shall be appointed by the Postmaster-General from among persons appearing to him to be qualified for the office, and of the members of the Authority other than the Chairman and Deputy Chairman three shall be persons who appear to the Postmaster-General to be suited to make the interests of Scotland, the interests of Wales and Monmouthshire and the interests of Northern Ireland, respectively, their special care.

*   *   *

2. -- (1) The Authority shall, subject to the provisions of this Act, have power to do all such things as are in their opinion necessary for or conducive to the proper discharge of their function as described in subsection (1) of section one of this Act, and, in particular and without prejudice to the generality of the foregoing provision, they shall for the purpose of discharging that function have power --

(a) to establish, install and use stations for wireless telegraphy;

(b) to arrange for the provision and equipment of, or, if need be, themselves to provide and equip, studios and other premises for television broadcasting purposes;

(c) by arrangements made for the purpose with the Postmaster-General and persons carrying on broadcast relay stations, to provide for the distribution from broadcast relay stations of programmes broadcast by the Authority.

(2) The programmes broadcast by the Authority shall, so far as may be consistent with the observance of the requirements of this Act, be provided not by the Authority but by persons (hereinafter in this Act referred to as "programme contractors") who, under contracts with the Authority, have, in consideration of payments to the Authority and subject to the provisions of this Act, the right and the duty to provide programmes or parts of programmes to be broadcast by the Authority, which may include advertisements; but the Authority may --

(a) arrange for the provision of parts of programmes otherwise than as aforesaid for the purpose of securing the inclusion in the programmes of items of particular classes which in their opinion are necessary for securing a proper balance in the subject matter of the programmes and cannot, or cannot as suitably, be provided by programme contractors; and

(b) apart from the provision of such items, arrange for the provision, otherwise than as aforesaid, of, or, if need be, themselves provide, programmes or parts of programmes so far as many be necessary be reason of any temporary lack of suitable persons able and willing to become or continue as programme contractors on suitable terms and to perform their obligations as such, or by reason of any interval between the expiration or termination of one contract with a programme contractor and the commencement of another contract with that or another programme contractor, . . .

THE LIFE PEERAGES ACT, April 30, 1958

Source: The Public General Acts and . . . Measures of 1958 (London: Her Majesty's Stationery Office, 1958) p. 84.

It was decided that it would be in the best interests of the nation to honor certain British subjects by granting them life peerages which would enable them to sit in the House of Lords and to contribute to the growth and development of Britain.

1958 CHAPTER 21

An Act to make provision for the creation of life peerages carrying the right to sit and vote in the House of Lords.

[30th April, 1958]

Be it enacted by the Queen's most Excellent Majesty, by and with the advice and consent of the Lords Spiritual and Temporal, and Commons, in this present Parliament assembled, and by the authority of the same, as follows: --

1. -- (1) Without prejudice to Her Majesty's powers as to the appointment of Lords of Appeal in Ordinary, Her Majesty shall have power by letters patent to confer on any person a peerage for life having the incidents specified in subsection (2) of this section.

(2) A peerage conferred under this section shall, during the life of the person on whom it is conferred, entitle him --

(a) to rank as a baron under such style as may be appointed by the letters patent; and

(b) subject to subsection (4) of this section, to receive writs of summons to attend the House of Lords and sit and vote therein accordingly,

and shall expire on his death.

(3) A life peerage may be conferred under this section on a woman.

(4) Nothing in this section shall enable any person to receive a writ of summons to attend the House of Lords, or to sit and vote in that House, at any time when disqualified therefor by law.

2. This Act may be cited as the Life Peerages Act, 1958.

BIBLIOGRAPHY

The works in this bibliography have been critically selected to present students with a variety of works as a basis for further research into the eras in the development of English history. Additional titles may be found in the bibliographies of the monographs and general histories listed below. Students might also wish to consult Historical Abstracts for recent articles in scholarly journals.

SOURCE MATERIALS

OFFICIAL SOURCES

British and Foreign State Papers, 1812/14 ff. London, 1841 ff. (Twentieth
    Century Volumes published by H. M. Stationery Office)
    Contains various treaties, conventions, and agreements as well as
    documents which in any way pertain to foreign affairs. In addition
    some specific British Acts and Proclamations are included.

Ford, Grace, and Percy Ford, eds. Guide to Parliamentary Papers, 2nd
    ed. Oxford, 1956.

--------------------------, eds. Hansard's Catalogue and Breviate of
    Parliamentary Papers, 1696-1834. Oxford: Basil Blackwell & Mott,
    Ltd., 1953.

Gooch, George P. and Howard W. V. Temperley, eds. British Documents
    on the Origins of the War, 1898-1914. 11 vols. London, 1926-1938.

Great Britain. Public Record Office. Calendar of State Papers. London:
    Longmans, Green & Co., Ltd., and others, 1856 ff. This series
    covers domestic, foreign, and colonial affairs as well as various
    charters and patents.

Hansard, Thomas C. The Parliamentary Debates. London, 1804 ff. 5
    series. This along with the Parliamentary History of England listed
    below covers the daily proceedings of Parliament.

Hertslet, Lewis, Sir Edward Hertslet, et. al., eds. A complete Collection
    of the Treaties, Conventions, and Reciprocal Regulations at Present
    Subsisting Between Great Britain and Foreign Powers. 19 vols. Lon-
    don, 1827-1894.

Parliamentary History of England from the Norman Conquest in 1066 to the

Year 1803. ed. by William Cobbett. 36 vols. London, 1806-1820. Reprint New York: AMS Press, 1966.

Public General Statutes. London, 1832-1867.

Public General Acts of the United Kingdom of Great Britain and Ireland. London, 1887 ff. This series and the preceding contain all acts passed in the periods involved to the present day.

The Statutes at Large, from Magna Charta to the end of the Last Parliament of Great Britain, held in the 41st year of the Reign of King George III, 1800. 14 vols. London, 1786-1800.

Tomlins, Thomas E., et. al., eds. The Statutes at Large of the United Kingdom of Great Britain and Ireland, 29 vols. London, 1804-69. (Titles vary).

DOCUMENTARY COLLECTIONS

Barker, William A., et. al., eds. A General History of England: Documents. 2 vols. London, 1952-53. Useful general collection from 1688 to 1850.

Bland, Alfred E., Philip A. Brown, and Richard H. Tawney, eds. English Economic History: Select Documents. London; G. Bell and Sons, Ltd., 1937. The only general work which contains a wide selection of economic sources.

Costin, William C. and J. Stevens Watson, eds. The Law and Working of the Constitution, 1660-1914. 2 vols. London, 1952.

Douglas, David C., ed. English Hisotrical Documents. Oxford: Oxford University Press, 1953 ff. Collection projected in 12 volumes. Well-chosen and carefully edited documents.

Dunham, William H. and Stanley M. Pargellis: Complaint and Reform in England, 1436-1714. New York: Octagon Books, 1968. This is a valuable collection of documents and sources in social and political history.

Gardiner, Samuel R. The Constitutional Documents of the Puritan Revolution, 1625-1660. Oxford: Clarendon Press, 1951.

Haller, William and Godfrey Davies, eds. The Leveller Tracts, 1647-1653. New York: Columbia University Press, 1944. Good selection of documents by the left-wing Puritans.

Keir, Sir David and Frederick H. Lason. Cases in Constitutional Law, 4th ed. Oxford: Oxford University Press, 1954. Useful casebook for constitutional law.

Lee, Guy C., ed. Source-Book of English History ... New York, H. Holt and Company, 1900. Fine selection of documents, papers and other materials.

LeMay, Godfrey H. L., ed. British Government, 1914-53; Select Documents. London: Methuen & Co., Ltd., 1955. Useful selection of government documents for the twentieth century.

Tanner, Joseph R., ed. Tudor Constitutional Documents, 1485-1603. Cambridge, England: The University Press, 1922. Carefully selected and well-edited documents of this era.

Tawney, Richard H. and Eileen Power, eds. Tudor Economic Documents. New ed. 3 vols. London: Longmans, Green & Co., Ltd., 1951.

THE TUDOR PERIOD

Bindoff, Stanley, T. Tudor England. Hammondsworth, Middlesex: Penguin Books, Inc., 1950. Concise general history of the Tudor Era. Pelican History of England vol. 5.

Cam, Helen M. England Before Elizabeth. London: The Hutchinson Publishing Group, Ltd., 1967. Interesting analysis of early Tudor period and what Elizabeth's inheritance was.

Chapman, Hester W. Lady Jane Grey, October 1537-February 1554. Boston: Little Brown and Company, 1963. Balanced picture indicating that Jane was not as innocent as formerly proclaimed.

Einstein, Lewis David. Tudor Ideals. London: G. Bell and Sons, Ltd., 1921. Analyzes spirit and tendency of the age. Little on political aspects.

Elton, Geoffrey Rudolph. England Under the Tudors. London: Methuen & Co., Ltd., 1955. Fine survey of the period, surpasses previous ones.

----------------------. The Tudor Revolution in Government: Administrative Changes in the Reign of Henry VIII. Cambridge: Cambridge University Press, 1953. Study of the change in the methods and principles of English government in the sixteenth period.

Feiling, Keith G. England Under the Tudors and Stuarts. London; H.
Holt & Company, 1935. Excellent survey.

Froude, James A. History of England from the Fall of Wolsey to the Death
of Elizabeth. 12 vols. New York: AMS Press, 1969. Last two volumes completed by Edward Cheney. Detailed history of the era by
the nineteenth century historian.

Graves, M. A. R. England Under the Tudors and Stewarts, 1485-1689.
London: G. Bell and Sons, Ltd., 1965

Harrison, David. Tudor England. London: Cassell & Company, Ltd.,
1953. Good analysis of the period.

Hurtsfield, Joel. The Elizabethan Nation. New York: Harper and Row,
Publishers, 1967. General discussion of various aspects of the Elizabethan world.

McCaffrey, Lawrence. The Irish Question, 1800-1922. Louisville, Kentucky: University of Kentucky Press, 1969. Analysis of evolution of
Irish nation since 1800 and its impact on British culture.

MacCaffrey, Wallace T. The Shaping of the Elizabethan Regime. Princeton, New Jersey: Princeton University Press, 1968. Indicates that the
years 1558-1572 were essential in helping to bridge the crisis of the
Tudor Century.

McGrath, Patrick. Papists and Puritans Under Elizabeth I. New York:
Walker & Company, 1967. Interesting analysis of the religious problems during the reign is presented.

Mackie, John Duncan. The Earlier Tudors, 1485-1558. Oxford: Clarendon
Press, 1952. Is part of the Oxford History. Excellent narrative account is developed.

Mattingly, Garrett. Catharine of Aragon. New York: Vintage Books, 1960.
The author has written a good solid biography of the Queen and her
problems.

-----------------. The Invincible Armada and Elizabethan England.
Ithaca, New York: Cornell University Press, 1963. This is an ex-
cellent analysis of England's relationship with Spain and other states.
It gives a fine description of preparation for and defeat of the Armada.

Maynard, Theodore. Humanist as Hero; the Life of Sir Thomas More.
Ithaca, New York: Cornell University Press, 1947. Proves More's

value; written from a Catholic viewpoint.

Neale, John E. Queen Elizabeth. New York: Harcourt, Brace & Company, 1934. This is an entertaining work about the Queen and London, one of best biographies of Elizabeth.

Pollard, Albert F. Henry VIII. New York: Longmans, Green & Co., Ltd., 1951. This is perhaps the best scholarly biography of the King.

----------------. Wolsey. New York: Longmans, Green & Co., Ltd., 1929. This is a good companion to Pollard's study of Henry VIII.

Prescott, Hilda F.M. Mary Tudor. New York: The Macmillan Company, 1953. A distinguished and fairminded comprehensive biography which is sympathetic to the Queen.

Read, Conyers. The Tudors; Personalities and Practical Politics in 16th century England. New York: H. Holt and Company, 1936. Well-balanced history of the era.

Rowse, Alfred I. The Elizabethans and America. New York: Harper and Row, Publishers, 1959. Informative work concerning the English voyage to America.

----------------. The England of Elizabeth; the Structure of Society. London: Macmillan & Company, Ltd., 1950. Fine portrait of Elizabethan age is developed.

Sitwell, Edith. Fanfare for Elizabeth. New York: The Macmillan Company, 1946. Picture of the England in which she was born, describing Henry VIII and his wives.

------------. The Queens and the Hive. Boston: Little, Brown and Company, 1962. Sequel to the work listed above, discussing the power and glory of sixteenth century England as well as the relationship of the Queen with Mary Tudor, Mary Stuart and Catharine de Medici.

Tawney, Richard H. Religion and the Rise of Capitalism. New York: Peter Smith, 1961. The theme is the influence of religious opinion on social ethics during the sixteenth and seventeenth centuries.

Williams, Charles Harold. The Making of Tudor Despotism. New York: Russell & Russell, Publishers, 1967. Is a fine analysis of the governmental developments under the Tudors.

THE STUARTS: 1603-1713

Ashley, Maurice P. Cromwell's Generals. New York: St. Morton's Press, Inc., 1955. Presents a biographical analysis of Cromwell's supporters.

----------------. England in the 17th Century. Baltimore: Penguin Books, Inc., 1961. Fine general discussion of the entire era is developed in this work.

----------------. The Glorious Revolution of 1688. New York: Charles Scribner's Sons, 1967. Presents analysis of the Revolution and the work of William III.

----------------. The Stuarts in Love. New York: The Macmillan Company, 1964. Discusses the royal love life as well as a general discussion of love and marriage in the seventeenth century.

----------------. The Greatness of Oliver Cromwell. New York: The Macmillan Company, 1958. Defender of Cromwell in a favorable account.

Belloc, Hilaire. Charles the First, King of England. Philadelphia: J. B. Lippincott Company, 1933. Fine study of the life and times of Charles, including an analysis of the aristocratic governing class.

Beloff, Max. Public Order and Popular Disturbances, 1660-1714. London: R. Cass, 1963. Study of popular discontent during this period indicating that it was not based on class consciousness.

Bosher, Robert S. The Making of the Restoration Settlement; The Influence of the Laudians, 1649-1662. Westminster, England: Dacre Press, 1951. Is standard reference on the subject.

Bridenbaugh, Carl. Vexed and Troubled Englishmen, 1590-1642. New York: Oxford University Press, 1968. Study of the common people, surveying every aspect of life.

Bryant, Sir Arthur. King Charles II, 2nd ed. London: Longmans, Green and Company, Ltd., 1955. It is most useful general biography.

Buchan, John. Oliver Cromwell. Boston: Houghton Mifflin Company, 1934. This popular and well-documented work is a fine discussion.

Campbell, Mrs. Kathleen W. Sarah, Duchess of Marlborough. Boston:

Little, Brown and Company, 1932. This is an excellent study of the woman.

Churchill, Winston L. S. Marlborough, His Life and Times. 6 vols. New York: Charles Scribner's Sons, 1933-38. This ambitious work by the descendant of John Churchill has a detailed analysis.

Clark, Sir. George N. The Later Stuarts, 1660-1714. Oxford: Clarendon Press, 1955. Is fine well-balanced discussion of the era.

Davies, Godfrey. The Early Stuarts, 1603-1660. Oxford: Clarendon Press, 1937. This volume in the Oxford History of England is a fine account making good use of its sources.

----------------. Essays on the Later Stuarts. San Marino, California: Henry E. Huntington Library & Art Gallery, 1958. These are fine contributions concerning Charles II and James II.

----------------. The Restoration of Charles II, 1658-1660. San Marino, California: Henry E. Huntington Library & Art Gallery, 1955. This is valuable for its explanations of the reasons for the Restoration.

Firth, Sir Charles H. Oliver Cromwell and the Rule of the Puritans in England. New York: G. P. Putnam's Sons, 1924.

Hexter, Jack H. The Reign of King Pym. Cambridge, Mass: Harvard University Press, 1941. Good discussion of this Parliamentary leader and party organization.

Hill, Christopher. The Century of Revolution, 1603-1714. Edinburgh: Thomas Nelson & Sons, Ltd., 1961. Good description of the era, studying the role of religion, politics, the middle class, and monarch.

----------------. Intellectual Origins of the English Revolution. Oxford: Clarendon Press, 1965. Explores events of the Revolution in relation to the writings of Bacon, Raleigh, Coke and others.

----------------. Puritanism and Revolution: Studies in Interpretation of the English Revolution of the 17th Century. New York: Schocken Books, 1964. Good scholarly study of the aspects of the Revolution.

Holmes, Geoffrey S. British Politics in the Age of Anne. New York: St. Morton's Press, 1968. Analyzes the struggle for supremacy of two great parties.

Kenyon, John P. The Stuarts; A Study in English Kingship. London: B.

T. Batsford, Ltd., 1958. Fine sketches of the sovereigns are presented.

Macaulay, Thomas Babington. The History of England from the Accession of James the Second. 10 vols. New York: G. P. Putnam's Sons, 1898. This is an important analysis of English history.

Notestein, Wallace. The English People on the Eve of Colonization. New York: Harper and Row, Publishers, 1954. Excellent over-all study of social history in the period.

Ogg, David. England in the Reigns of James II and William III. Oxford: Clarendon Press, 1950.

----------. William III. New York: The Macmillan Company, 1956. Presents him as a figure who contributed to the advancement of the state.

Pinkham, Lucile. William III and the Respectable Revolution; the Part Played by William of Orange in the Revolution of 1688. Cambridge, Mass: Harvard University Press, 1954. Is important for any study of the period.

Schenk, William. The Concern for Social Justice in the Puritan Revolution. New York: Longmans, Green & Co., Ltd., 1948. Excellent study of social radical movements.

Taylor, George Robert S. Cromwell. Boston: Little, Brown and Company, 1928. Provocative study characterizing his character and career.

Trevelyan, George M. England Under Queen Anne. 5 vols. New York: Longmans, Green & Co., Ltd., 1930-34. Detailed discussion of all aspects of politics and diplomacy is presented.

--------------------. The English Revolution, 1688-1689. London: T. Butterworth, Ltd., 1938. Uses basic material to bring out factors leading up to and during the Revolution.

--------------------. England Under the Stuarts. New York: Barnes & Noble Books, 1949. Is a fine study of the seventeenth century and good analysis of the Kings.

Underdown, David. Royalist Conspiracy in England, 1649-1660. New Haven: Yale University Press, 1960. Story of devotion and failure of the Royalist party who worked for the return of the monarchy.

Wedgwood, Cicely V. The King's Peace, 1637-1641. New York: The Mac-

millan Company, 1955. Fine analysis of the beginnings of the troubles.

------------------. Poetry and Politics Under the Stuarts. Cambridge,
England: University Press, 1960.

Willson, David Harris. King James VI and I. New York: Oxford University Press, Inc., 1967. Presents fine analysis of the first of the
Stuarts.

Wilson, John Harold. A Rake and His Times: George Villiers, 2nd Duke
of Buckingham. New York: Farrar, Straus and Young, 1954.

Wolfe, Don Marion. Milton and His England. Princeton: Princeton University Press, 1971.

THE GEORGIAN ERA: 1714-1837

Aldington, Richard. Wellington, Being an Account of the Life and Achieve-
ments of Arthur Wellesley, First Duke of Wellington. London: Wm.
Heinemann, Ltd., 1946.

Briggs, Asa. The Age of Improvement, 1783-1867. London: Longmans,
Green & Co., Ltd., 1960. Has developed a fine analysis of the social and political change during this period.

Bryant, Sir Arthur. The Years of Endurance, 1793-1802. London: William
Collins & Sons & Co., Ltd., 1940. Is useful survey of Britain during
the wars of the French Revolution and Napoleon.

------------------. The Years of Victory, 1802-1812. London: William
Collins Sons & Co., Ltd., 1944. A good survey of victorious struggle with Napoleonic France is presented in this volume.

Butterfield, Herbert. George III, Lord North and the People, 1779-1780.
London: G. Bell and Sons, Ltd., 1949.

Derry, John Wesley. Reaction and Reform, 1793-1868. England in the
Early 19th Century. New York: Humanities Press, Inc., 1968. Analyzes activities and motives of reformers and their opponents.

------------------. The Regency Crisis and the Whigs, 1788-9. Cambridge, England: Humanities Press, Inc., 1963. Shows that this political crisis was the first stage in the break-up of the old Whig party.

Eyck, Erich. Pitt versus Fox: Father and Son, 1735-1806. trans. by E.

Northcott. London: G. Bell and Sons, Ltd., 1950. Is fine on elder
Pitt.

Fay, Charles R. Huskisson and His Age. New York: Longmans, Green,
& Co., Ltd., 1951. Gives interesting impressions of the man and his
role in politics.

Gipson, Lawrence Henry. The British Empire Before the American Revolution... 8 vols. New York: Alfred A. Knopf, Inc., 1936-1953.
Presents a carefully integrated and copiously documented study of
the British Empire.

Greville, Charles Cavendish Fulke. The Great World; Portraits and
Scenes from Greville's Memoirs, 1814-1860. Garden City, New York:
Doubleday Publishing Company, 1963. Louis Kronenberger made the
selections for the eight volumes involved.

Guedella, Philip. Palmerston, 1784-1865. New York: G.P. Putnam's
Sons, 1927. Gives great detail in this interesting account.

Halevy, Elie. A History of the English People in the 19th Century. Trans.
from the French by E. I. Watking and D. A. Barker. 6 vols., New
York: Peter Smith, 1949-1952. Fine detailed account of the century
by this Frenchman.

Harlow, Vincent Todd. The Founding of the Second British Empire, 1763-
1793. New York: Longmans, Green & Co., Ltd., 1952. Interesting
discussion showing that Britain did not remain inactive after lost
American colonies.

Jones, Louis Clark. The Clubs of the Georgian Rakes. New York: Columbia University Press, 1942. Is interesting study of these specific
clubs for social purposes.

Long, John Cuthbert. Mr. Pitt and America's Birthright; A Biography of
William Pitt, the Earl of Chatham, 1708-1778. New York: Stokes,
1940.

Mackesy, Piers. The War for America, 1775-1783. Cambridge, Massachusetts: Harvard University Press, 1964. British view of the American war is presented.

Marshall, Dorothy. Eighteenth Century England. New York: David Mc-
Kay Co., Inc., 1962. This is fine introduction to the period.

Namier, Lewis Bernstein. England in the Age of the American Revolution.

London: Macmillan & Company, Ltd., 1930. Excellent intellectual and political view of England is developed.

Pares, Richard. George III and the Politicians. Oxford: Clarendon Press, 1953. Presents a good discussion of George's political influence.

Petrie, Sir Charles A. The Four Georges: A Revaluation of the Period from 1714-1830. Port Washington, N.Y.: Kennikat Press, 1971. Shows how people lived and viewed problems.

Plumb, John Harold. The First Four Georges. New York: The Macmillan Company, 1957. Presents interesting character sketches.

------------------. Sir Robert Walpole, vol. I. The Making of a Statesman. Boston: Houghton Mifflin Company, 1956. Is important work on the man.

Quinlan, Maurice J. Victorian Prelude; A History of English Manners, 1700-1830. New York: Columbia University Press, 1941. Presents a challenging analysis of religious and social developments.

Seeley, Walter T. England in the 18th Century. London: A. & C. Black, Ltd., 1964. Is a good general discussion of the century.

Temperley, Harold W.V. The Foreign Policy of Canning, 1822-1827; England, the Neo-Holy Alliance, and the New World. Hamden, Conn.: Anchor Books, 1966. Good discussion of the role of Canning in shaping England's foreign policy in the 1820's is presented.

Thomson, David. England in the 19th Century, 1815-1914. Middlesex: Penguin Books, Inc., 1950.

Trevelyan, George M. British History in the Nineteenth Century and After (1782-1919). New York: Longmans, Green & Co., Ltd., 1958. Presents a fine analysis of the period.

Tuberville, Arthur S. English Men and Manners in the 18th Century, an Illustrative Narrative. Oxford: Clarenden Press, 1932. Fine political, social, cultural, and religious analysis is presented.

Watson, John S. The Reign of George III, 1760-1815. Oxford: Clarenden Press, 1960. Emphasizes complexities of party politics.

White, Reginald J. Waterloo to Peterloo. New York: David White Company, 1957. Good interpretation of the social and intellectual change in this period is developed.

Williams, Basil. The Whig Supremacy, 1714-1760. Oxford: Clarendon
    Press, 1942. Is a good addition to the Oxford History of England.

Williams, E. Neville. Life in Georgian England. New York: B. T. Bats-
    ford Ltd., 1962. Presents good discussion of the society of the times.

Wood, Anthony. Nineteenth Century Britain, 1815-1914. London: Longmans,
    Green & Co., Ltd., 1960. Good general history illustrates the high-
    lights of the period.

Woodward, Ernest L. The Age of Reform, 1815-1870. Oxford: Clarendon
    Press, 1938. Presents good survey of political, economic and social
    history.

THE VICTORIAN ERA

Briggs, Asa. Victorian Cities. London: Oldhams Books, 1964. Fine study
    of the important urban centers, as well as social life and views of
    the Victorians is developed.

-----------. Victorian People; A Reassessment of Persons and Themes,
    1851-67, revised ed., Chicago: University of Chicago Press, 1970.
    Informative essays present a good picture of part of the era.

British Broadcasting Corporation. Ideas and Beliefs of the Victorians; An
    Historic Revaluation of the Victorian Age. London: Sylvan Press,
    1949. Varied essays broadcast give important insights.

Burn, William Laurence. The Age of Equipoise; A Study of the Mid-Vic-
    torian Generation. New York: W. W. Norton & Company, Inc., 1964.
    Important study presents information of English thought between 1852
    and 1867.

Cruikshank, Robert J. Charles Dickens and Early Victorian England. Lon-
    don: Sir Isaac Pitman & Sons, Ltd., 1949. Presents a study of life
    and customs from 1837 to 1870.

Dangerfield, George. The Strange Death of Liberal England. New York:
    G. P. Putnam's Sons, 1961. Important work on the decline of the
    party before 1914.

Davis, Henry W. C. The Age of Grey and Peel. Oxford: Clarendon Press,
    1929.

Ensor, Robert C. K. England, 1870-1914. Oxford: Clarendon Press, 1936.
    Is excellent volume in the Oxford History of England series.

Evans, Joan. The Victorians. London: Cambridge University Press, 1966. Presents a fine sequence of pictures and extracts from the writings of the Victorians.

Grenville, J. A. S. Lord Salisbury and Foreign Policy; the Close of the 19th Century. London: Athlone Press, 1964. This study is concerned with readjustment of the British foreign policy from 1895 to 1902.

Guedella, Philip. The Queen and Mr. Gladstone. New York: 1969.

Hammond, John L. and Barbara Hammond. The Age of the Chartists, 1832-1854. New York: Longmans, Green and Co., Ltd., 1930. Presents best brief social and political history of the era.

Kitson, Clark George. Peel and the Conservative Party, London: F. Cass, 1964. Is important study of Peel's influence.

Low, Sir Sidney James M. and Lloyd C. Sanders. The History of England During the Reign of Victoria (1837-1901). New York: Longmans, Green. & Co., Ltd., 1969.

Magnus, Sir Philip M. Gladstone, A Biography. New York: E. P. Dutton & Co., Inc., 1954. Fine addition to basic knowledge of the man.

Martin, Robert B. Enter Rumor; Four Early Victorian Scandals. New York: 1962. Entertaining discussion of scandals.

Morely, John. The Life of William Ewart Gladstone. New York: The Macmillan Company, 1968. Is good early biography first published in 1903.

Morris, James. Pax Britannica; the Climax of an Empire. New York: Harcourt Brace, Jovanovich, 1968. Captures the brilliance and squalor of the time.

Pelling, Henry. Modern Britain, 1885-1955. Edinburgh: Thomas Nelson Inc., 1960. Good general history explaining various aspects is developed.

Pike, Edgar R. Golden Times; Human Documents of the Victorian Age. New York: Praeger Publishers, Inc., 1967. Fine study developed through documents.

--------------. Hard Times; Human Documents of the Industrial Revolution. New York: Praeger Publishers, Inc., 1966. Collection of various extracts from official reports is presented.

Strachey, Lytton. Eminent Victorians: Cardinal Manning, Florence
    Nightingale, Dr. Arnold, General Gordon. London: G. P. Putnam's
    Sons, 1918. Presents an interesting picture and criticism of the era.

Trevelyan, George M. Lord Grey of the Reform Bill. London: Longmans,
    Green & Co., Ltd., 1920.

Woodham-Smith, Mrs. Cecil Blanche. Queen Victoria: From Her Birth to
    the Death of the Prince Constort. New York: Alfred A. Knopf, Inc.,
    1972. Good discussion of family life is presented.

Young, George M. Victorian England: Portrait of an Age. New York: Ox-
    ford University Press, 1953.

THE TWENTIETH CENTURY

Ashworth, William. An Economic History of England, 1870-1938. London:
    Barnes & Noble Books, 1960. Solid study which uses economic infor-
    mation available.

Beer, Samuel. British Politics in the Collectivist Age. New York: Alfred
    Knopf Inc., 1965. Shows how the old Whig and Tory politics evolved
    into the Labour and Conservative parties.

Beveridge, William. Full Employment in a Free Society. New York: W.
    W. Norton & Company, Inc., 1945. The author proposes the method
    for dealing with unemployment in peacetime.

Blake, Robert. Unrepentant Tory: The Life and Times of Andrew Bonar
    Law, 1858-1923, Prime Minister of the United Kingdom. New York:
    St. Martin's Press, 1956. Good objective biography presents a fine
    analysis of the times.

Bolitho, Hector. King Edward VIII. An Intimate Biography. Philadelphia:
    J. B. Lippincott Company, 1937. Indicates the attitude of the people.

Brand, Carl F. The British Labour Party: A Short History. Stanford,
    California: Stanford University Press, 1964. Indicates the philosophy
    of the Party.

Briffault, Robert. The Decline and Fall of the British Empire. New York:
    Simon and Schuster, Inc., 1938. Denounces much of what Britain has
    done.

Butler, James R. M. A History of England, 1815-1939. 2nd ed. New York:
    Oxford University Press, 1960.

Churchill, Winston. Memoirs: The Second World War. New York: 1959
Presents a fine account of the war.

Cross, Colin. The Fall of the British Empire, 1918-1968. New York:
Coward-McCann, 1969. Impartial account points out the major issues.

Feiling, Keith. The Life of Neville Chamberlain. London: Macmillan &
Company, Ltd., 1946. Good biography which uses all available material.

Graves, Robert and Alan Hodge. The Long Weekend; A Social History of
Great Britain, 1918-1939. New York: The Macmillan Company, 1941.
Indicates the manners and customs of the English people, covering
almost every aspect of life.

James, Robert R. Rosebery. A Biography of Archibald Philip, 5th Earl
of Rosebery. New York: The Macmillan Company, 1963. Emphasizes domestic and social life.

Jenkins, Roy. Asquith. New York: Chilmark Press Inc., 1964.

Jones, Thomas. Lloyd George, Cambridge, Mass: Harvard University
Press, 1951. Presents a fine objective picture of many aspects of his
career.

Knaplund, Paul. Britain: Commonwealth and Empire, 1901-1955. New
York: Harper & Row, Publishers, 1957. Presents good interpreta-
tive study of British policy.

McBriar, A. M. Fabian Socialism and English Politics, 1884-1918. Cambridge, England: University Press, 1962. Presents the most comprehensive analysis dealing with the doctrine, organization and individual members.

Magnus, Philip. King Edward the Seventh. New York: E. P. Dutton &
Co., Inc., 1964. This is a good objective analysis.

Marwick, Arthur H. The Deluge, British Society and the First World War.
London: 1965. Analyzes life during the war and what changes occurred..

Mowat, Charles Loch. Britain Between the Wars, 1918-1940. Chicago:
University of Chicago Press, 1955. Studies all details of this com-
plicated era.

Nicolson, Harold. King George the Fifth: His Life and Reign. Garden

City, New York: Doubleday Publishing Company, 1953.

Taylor, Alan J. P. English History, 1914-1945. New York: Oxford University Press, 1965. Covers the two wars and the Depression presenting a fine condensation of material.

Thompson, David. England in the Twentieth Century, 1914-63. Baltimore: Penguin Books, 1965. This volume in the Penguin series presents a good summary of the period.

Wheeler-Bennett, John W. King George VI, His Life and Reign. New York: St. Martin's Press, 1968. This official biography tells the story of the King's triumph over his weaknesses.

Wolfers, Arnold. Britain and France Between Two Wars. New York: Harcourt, Brace and Company, 1940. Presents a valuable study of the causes of the war.

Young, Kenneth. Arthur James Balfour. The Happy Life of the Policitican, Prime Minister, Statesman and Philosopher, 1848-1930. London: G. Bell and Sons, Ltd., 1963.

186

Paxton, Sir Joseph, 47
Peel, Lord, 69
Peel, Robert, 44, 45, 46, 47
Penn, William, 23
Peter, Regent of Portugal, 44
Philip, King of Castile, 2
Philip I, King of Spain, 10
Philip II, King of Spain, 23
Philip, Prince (Duke of Edinburgh
  and husband of Elizabeth II), 78,
  85, 90
Philip of Anjou, 28
Pitt, William, 33, 34, 36
Pitt, William the Younger, 36, 38
Pole, Reginald Cardinal, 6, 11
Pope, Alexander, 30, 32
Pride, Colonel, 21
Profumo, John, 88
Pym, John, 20

Raleigh, Walter, 17
Rhodes, Cecil, 56
Richmond, Duke of, 3
Rizzio, David, 12
Rodjestvensky, Admiral, 58
Rooke, Sir George (Admiral), 29
Roosevelt, Franklin D. (U.S.
  President), 67, 72, 73, 74, 75, 76
Rosebery, Lord, 56
Ruskin, John, 46, 47
Russell, Bertrand, 92
Russell, Lord John, 45, 46

Sacheverell, Rev. Henry, 30
Sadler, Sir Ralph, 13
Salisbury, Lord, 54, 55, 58
Samuel, Sir Herbert, 65
Sandys, Duncan, 82
Saye, Lord, 18
Scott, Sir Walter, 39, 40
Seymour, Edward, 8
Seymour, Jane, Queen, 6
Seymour, Thomas (Lord Protec-
  tor Somerset), 9, 10
Shakespeare, William, 15, 16
Simpson, Mrs. Wallis Warfield
  (Duchess of Windsor), 68
Slidell, John, 50
Smith, Adam, 36

Smollett, Tobias, 33
Smuts, General, 70
Sophia, Electress of Hanover, 28
Stalin, Josef, 75, 76
Steele, Richard, 29, 30
Stephenson, George, 40
Strachy, John, 77
Strafford, Earl of, 19
Strode, William, 20
Swift, Jonathan, 31
Swinburne, Algernon Charles, 50

Tennyson, Alfred Lord, 47, 49
Thackeray, William Makepeace,47,48
Thistlewood, Francis, 41
Throckmorton, Francis, 14
Tindal, Matthew, 32
Tonge, Dr. Israel, 25
Townshend, Viscount Charles, 32
Trevelyan, Sir George, 54
Trollope, Anthony, 48
Truman, Harry S. (U.S. Presi-
  dent), 76
Tudor, Margaret, 2

Vane, Henry, 18
Venables, General Robert, 23
Victoria, Queen, 45, 46, 52, 55,
  57
Villiers, George, 17

Waltham, Lord, 4
Warbeck, Perkin, 2
Warren, Commodore Peter, 33
Warwick, Earl of, 2
Washington, George, 36
Wellington, Duke of, 42, 43
Weymouth, Viscount, 35
Wilkes, John, 34, 35
William II, German Emperor, 56
William III, 25, 27, 28, 29
William IV, 43, 45
Wilson, Harold, 89, 90, 91, 92
Wilson, Woodrow (U.S. President),62
Wolfe, General James, 34
Wolsey, Thomas, 3, 4
Wood, William, 31
Wordsworth, William, 38, 47
Wriothesley, Thomas, 8